ALWAYS SMiLE

CARLEY ALLISON'S
SECRETS FOR LAUGHING,
LOVING AND LIVING

BY ALICE KUIPERS

KCP Loft

Kids Can Press gratefully acknowledges the financial support of the Government of Ontario, through Ontario Creates; the Ontario Arts Council; the Canada Council for the Arts; and the Government of Canada for our publishing activity.

Published in Canada and the U.S. by Kids Can Press Ltd.
25 Dockside Drive, Toronto, ON M5A 0B5

Kids Can Press is a Corus Entertainment Inc. company

www.kidscanpress.com

The text is set in Minion Pro and Pompadour.

Photo credits:
Every reasonable effort has been made to trace ownership of, and give accurate credit to, copyrighted material. Information that would enable the publisher to correct any discrepancies in future editions would be appreciated.
Page 10, 19, 34, 59, 62, 81, 129, 177, 180, 208, 209, 211, 216, 227, 235, 263, 271, 277, 286, 300, 341, 348, 350: Mark Allison
Page 27, 60, 102, 134, 155, 156, 182, 259, 335: Riley Allison
Page 183, 273, 287: Ioannis Servinis
Page 179, 312: Carley Allison
Page 298: Sarah Fisher

Edited by Kate Egan
Designed by Emma Dolan

Printed and bound in Altona, Manitoba, Canada in 1/19 by Friesens

CM 19 0 9 8 7 6 5 4 3 2 1

Library and Archives Canada Cataloguing in Publication

Kuipers, Alice, 1979–, author
    Always smile : Carley Allison's secrets for laughing, loving and living
/ Alice Kuipers.
ISBN 978-1-5253-0040-0 (hardcover)

    1. Allison, Carey, 1995-2015 — Juvenile literature. 2. Trachea — Cancer — Patients — Canada — Biography — Juvenile literature. 3. Cancer — Patients — Canada — Biography — Juvenile literature. I. Title.

RC280.T5K85 2019   j362.19699'4230092   C2018-904422-5

It's not about how long you live,
but how you spend the time
while you are alive.

— **Carley**

ALICE KUIPERS, author

I never met Carley Allison. In fact, I didn't even know her name until it showed up in my inbox one day, a story in search of a writer. I did not know that she was a skater or a singer. I did not know that she had a magical life, filled with people who loved her and everything a girl could ever wish for. I did not know that she'd been diagnosed with a rare cancer, that she'd fought it bravely or inspired countless people or that she'd died too young. But I have come to know these things about Carley — and so much more — from spending many months immersed in the life she left behind.

To tell Carley's story, I drew heavily on the blog she wrote over the years of her illness. I've added the occasional word or sentence to clarify, but these are Carley's own words and own writing style, and her real thoughts on living with her diagnosis and treatment. Carley began her blog as an assignment because her illness meant she was missing so much school. She quickly realized that people found inspiration from her words, and so she kept on writing.

I also drew on the time I spent with Carley's family, who opened their doors to me and shared everything they could of Carley's: her videos, her songs, her photos, her texts, her posts. They introduced me to Carley's wide circle of friends and to John, the boy Carley loved. You will hear all their voices here, edited for length and clarity, telling all the facets of Carley's story and showing the wide range of lives she touched. You will also experience the world through Carley's eyes in scenes I have constructed from stories her family told me.

At the moment of her diagnosis, a vibrant and dynamic — but ordinary — young woman became extraordinary. Carley took the terrible thing that was happening to her and managed to keep her spirit and joy alive. She showed everyone around her how to live life to its fullest.

Carley lived according to simple rules that come up again and again in her blog or in the memories of the people who loved her. Above all, her secret to a happy life was this: Always smile.

This book begins with Carley's voice, just as it sounds in an interview she recorded with her father when her cancer was in remission. Carley and her dad set this up as if it were a media interview — it was a fun way to hang out together, but also an important record of how far Carley had come. After months of uncertainty and fear, they're relaxed in their living room at home. Carley is elegant in black, and you'd never guess what she's just been through. Because she is smiling. Always smiling.

CARLEY

Hey, everyone. My name's Carley Allison, and I'm going to tell you a little bit about my cancer story.

My everyday life before I was diagnosed was very busy. I was a competitive figure skater, musician and full-time student in school. My schedule was always very go-go-go. Then I got sick. My pathology was a clear cell sarcoma in the trachea. I was the second known case of this in the world — a one in 3.5 billion chance. Might as well buy a lottery ticket.

So, for me, one day I woke up and was like, Oh, wow, this is my reality now. I had to be pulled out of school, I wasn't skating and I couldn't sing. Singing was my best outlet, and I couldn't imagine my life without it.

My illness greatly affected my family. I'm just so grateful for all the things they did for me.

I'm grateful, too, for John.

My illness changed me 100 percent. My eyes have been opened. Before, if I was to see someone going through cancer, I'd say the typical things: Keep your head up. There's always light at the end of the tunnel.

But after going through it, I can say I know it's hard. I know it seems like there's never an end. Especially chemo. It feels exhausting. But never, never put doubts in your mind. Never think, Oh, well, I'm really, really not feeling well. Always think, Tomorrow I'll be better than I was today.

I still don't look up and think, Oh, I have cancer. It's not something I think about. When someone says it, it catches me off guard. Because I feel okay. In fact, I feel strong. And you never know how strong you are until strong is your only option.

CHAPTER ONE

Always be the best you can be.
— Carley

CARLEY

I'm just back from a fun day at the lake with Kat, Sydney, Denzelle and Jill. Those girls kill me — I never laughed so hard. On the drive back today, I played Taylor Swift and we all sang out the open windows, the wind through our hair, me dancing even while I drove, with shoulder shimmies, the open road before us filled with possibility.

Now I'm working on a song in the music room in our house. I scribble:

"Oh, I don't want you to go.
I want you to stay here, stay here with me.
Seems like every day we're coming closer to the day
when you will pack your bags and say ..."

always smile #maketodayyourbestday

This music room is one of my favorite places to be. Dad built this house — he's a contractor with his own business — and Mom did all the interiors. Mom and Dad met when they were in high school. I can't even imagine them young like that, getting married. I love thinking about what I'll wear when I get married one day: a white bikini on a sandy beach, perhaps.

Mom has gorgeous taste — think a home-and-decorating magazine and you've pretty much got a picture. Except, our house always smells like muffins — Mom makes twelve every day to feed us and our friends and our huge extended family, who love to swing by, especially my cousins, like Jeffrey. Mom makes these daily muffins just after she heads out for her morning run and just before she goes to work. Mom used to take me to her car dealership when I was a baby — maybe I'd like to work there one day. It's in my blood.

I pick up my guitar. We have five guitars — I know, we have a lot. We're lucky. I strum a few chords and open my mouth to sing.

I can never decide if I love to skate or to sing more. I sing a song I wrote recently:

"So I can wake up and feel if this is real.
Even when I'm gone, I know you'll think of me,
so hold me close and tell me that you'll always love me.
I'm just not good with goodbyes."

My boyfriend messages. Well, my on-and-off boyfriend. Right now, we're off. I delete his message without reading it. Whatever he has to say, I don't have time for it right now. Denzelle messages me a photo of us smiling together.

I message her:

> **Young, wild and free hahahahaha**

She messages back:

> Exactly

I check the time — if I fit in a quick run now, maybe tonight I can do something fun with Den. Or maybe I'll just see if John wants to go to Dairy Queen.

♥

I'm singing as I pull up to John's house. I'm always nervous when I wait outside in Ricky — that's the name of my white Jeep. John isn't my boyfriend or anything, but still I want his mom to love me — she's just the sort of person you want to impress, and I stress about coming up to the house and knocking on the door, or just waiting in the Jeep. I message John to let him know I'm here. I'm not even sure why I care what his mom thinks, anyway.

The song finishes on my stereo — "Girls Just Wanna Have Fun." And John comes out. He's wearing a shirt and jeans, clean-cut as always. He lifts his chin and climbs into the passenger seat. I smile at him. "How's it going?"

"I'm ready for ice cream."

His voice is low, soft, but steady. I like his voice. He'd sound good if he could sing. Which he can't.

"You? Skor?" he says.

"Always." I drive up for the best view in Toronto. Every time we go there, he tells me it's the best view in Toronto at least once. As I drive, I tell him about skating today. Shin, my skating coach, was super hard on me — I get that he wants me to be the best I can be. I do. Because I want that, too. But sometimes I wish he'd be a bit less stern. Except, then Shin gives me a smile, and I know we both want the same thing — in those moments, I know I may not be there yet, but I'm closer than I was yesterday.

At Dairy Queen I order a Skor Blizzard and go to our spot. John is checking his phone, while I leave him inside waiting for our ice creams. I sit for a moment on the bench outside, looking out at the evening light over the valley beyond. It's so beautiful here — and as I sit, I start thinking in song lyrics: *"It's hard to see your face when it's a million miles away."*

John sits on the other side of the picnic table, opposite me.

"Are you messaging a girl?" I ask.

He shakes his head and laughs.

"You just need to find … No. Even better, I'm going to find you the right girl."

"Carley, stop."

He laughs again. I look at him critically — he's handsome, for sure. Dark hair, dark eyes. His eyes are kind. He is kind — the sort of guy who opens a door for someone who needs it, who helps a stranger with a heavy bag. You can see when you look into his eyes that he's smart, too. A book guy — I mean schoolbooks, not stories. He's too rooted in reality to have time for made-up stories. One of the best things about John is how real he is.

I lean forward earnestly. "I'm gonna introduce you to someone perfect. And I'll be so mad at you if you don't take her out."

"I'm not even interested," he says. "Let's look at the best view in Toronto, instead."

"I knew you'd say that."

He opens his arms out wide. He's right — exactly here is the best place to be. We're quiet watching the sunset.

"I care about you. I loved you." More lyrics float into my mind. I'll write them down later, sing them perhaps at my piano, share them with my older sister, Riley, who I often call "Ri." Sure, we haven't been hanging out as much as usual this

summer. I'm so busy with skating and my own friends. It's weird — we've always been more like best friends than sisters. I've always looked up to her, wanted to do everything she does. But she's been doing tons of stuff without me this summer, and I guess I'm mad at her. Not that I'd tell her that. Anyway, I'm too busy with my own life to care what she does with hers.

My ice cream is melting. I eat it quickly, chatting with John about the end of summer, about going back to school. Grade twelve is going to be the best year ever.

I'm so excited about skating and sectionals and prom — I'm going to get this dress with one shoulder on, one shoulder off, in silver. Can't wait.

As we get back in the Jeep, I start coughing.

"You sick?" John asks.

I shake my head. "Just this asthma. I'm on an inhaler. It's a bitch. Whatever. I'm not gonna let it stop me."

SAM SERVINIS, John's mom

That was the summer of Dairy Queen and Carley.

LYNDSAY REDDICK, Carley's friend

Carley and I first met when we were eleven years old, at a sleep-away camp named Saddlewood. We were assigned to the same cabin and immediately became friends. I still remember, over ten years later, watching Mark and May move her into our side-by-side bunk beds and thinking, Wow, this girl is way cooler than me. I'm going to make sure we become friends! From then on we were pretty much inseparable!

We became even closer when our older sisters, Riley and Jenny, became close friends. The four of us became this sort of sister gang — we considered one another family — we fought like sisters and loved one another like sisters.

SARAH FISHER, Carley's friend

The first time I saw Carley we were at Coffee House at our school, where people would regularly sing, dance, do anything that they liked to do and perform. And the first time I really saw Carley was in front of whoever was there at Coffee House. She was two years below me, and we hadn't really met yet. Carley was wearing her school uniform. And she was singing a Taylor Swift cover, and there was just this beautiful, gorgeous, perfect little blond girl with a guitar and this huge voice. Everyone was just cheering and was so in love with her, and she was such a small person, and she had such a big voice. And that was the first time.

HOLLY DE JONGE, family friend

In 2002 I started working as the nanny with the Allisons. I became part of the family, and now the family and I will be friends forever. They nicknamed me "Hol-Hol." I didn't spoil the kids a lot — it was tough love. I wanted to make sure we didn't spend lots of money. We'd walk to a cheaper parking spot. If the kids made crumbs at lunch, they would have to vacuum, and I'd get them to do chores around the house. I made little games of it.

I knew Carley all through school, junior high school. I'd see her for lunch and after school. We had lots of adventures together — we loved walking the family dog together. Jack was an incredible dog. We used to do lots of arts and crafts, and we were always making things for their parents.

Many days, I'd get to the house and Carley would mimic me and put on the same clothes. She was a really happy kid, and she had a really natural athletic talent. She loved running and skating. At track meets she'd always be way ahead of the other kids, and she was very competitive. Her natural talent shone, and I think she got that from her mom, who was an Olympic marathon runner.

success will happen when you want it as badly as you want to breathe

SHIN AMANO, Carley's skating coach

When she stepped on the ice, she started to smile. Always. I could see through her face that she appreciated being on the ice and being able to skate. People forget how amazing it is to be on the ice and how amazing it feels, but her smile — I'll never forget it.

MAY, RILEY and SAMANTHA ALLISON,
Carley's mother and sisters

RILEY: There are two scores in skating. It was impossible to get a 50/50 split between your Components score and your Technical score. Carley would almost always achieve a 50/50 split because her skating skills were so high compared to the girls at her level. She could skate beautifully. And if she landed all her jumps, she'd win. It's hard. You've got to land — you've got to leave the ice, do two to two and a half to three rotations and land on the size of a dime. That's all you have.

SAMANTHA: And if your foot is even a little bit not straight, you fall. Carley was amazing. She was very expressive, a very good skater. But if she ever didn't land all the jumps, I'd try to say, "That was beautiful."

Carley would be, like, "Yeah, okay."

But she's giving me a look.

I was just, like, "What did I do? Who did I kill?"

MAY: In skating you have to do these athletic things, thinking about what's next, how you will land it, if you did it correctly, all the while making it look as if you are dancing effortlessly to music.

RILEY: I think that's why she loved it.

CARLEY

Kat shows up at my door and holds out a wrapped gift. She says, "I got this for you!"

Kat is tall, dark haired, athletic. We love to talk about running or skating or volleyball, or just hang out post-workout. None of our other friends ever want to talk about anything to do with sports, so I just adore hanging out with her.

"What's this for?" I ask her.

"I missed your birthday while I was away at training."

I rip open the pretty package. It's a beautiful white sweater from Aritzia. "Oh, it's gorgeous, Kat. Thanks!" I hold it up against myself. "I should wear it tonight. It's perfect."

"It suits you. Good. I thought it would. We should get ready. We'll be late for Jill and Den. Except, I don't even know what to wear." She heads into my bathroom to try on both the outfits she's brought as options to wear. I hear her sigh.

"You okay?" I join her in the bathroom and start to put waves into my hair. I watch in the mirror over my sink as she changes again.

"Wow. I don't look good in anything."

"That top makes you look great," I reply. I hold my curling iron and wink at her in the mirror.

"*Urgh*. This is putting me in a bad mood. I don't even want to go anymore."

"We're going to have a great time. You're beautiful," I say. I place the curling iron on the edge of the sink and turn to her. "You know what, Kat? This sweater you got me would look SO good on you. You should wear it."

"Really? No. I just got it for you."

"Seriously — it's going to be perfect."

KAT TSIOFAS, Carley's friend

Although the sweater was a little small because Carley was a lot shorter than me (she was a figure skater and I was a volleyball player), I did like it and ended up wearing it to the party. It was a small gesture, but that's just the type of friend Carley was. She was always looking out for everyone else.

CARLEY

By the time I get back from my run, I'm full of energy. I love the feeling running gives me. Love it and hate it — running competitively made me push myself so hard it made me feel sick, so I'm not competing as much anymore. I have some cross-country stuff coming up in the fall, but I've mainly decided to focus on skating.

I eat one of Mom's banana-chocolate-chip muffins and grab my stuff for skating. I'm due on the ice pretty soon. I message Sarah to see if she wants to hang out later. My big sister, Ri, is home for the weekend, and she glances up from her computer to smile at me.

"Good run?"

"It's nice out."

"Do you miss it? Running, I mean."

"Not really." She's talking about when I used to run in stuff like the Ontario Federation of School Athletic Associations — OFSAA. I was twenty-first in Ontario in cross-country. You'd think that doing so well would make me want to keep up with running, but I don't love it the way I love to skate. I'm about to tell Ri all this — I think about the millions of conversations we've had, curled up together in our den or on the couches that run like wide train tracks from the kitchen to our huge fireplace. After family parties or when Lyndsay and Jenny come over. I miss all that so much.

She's already looking back at her computer. I get the same feeling of irritation I've been getting recently every time I see her. I know it's partly my fault, but I wish we could go back to how we used to be. Ri and I did most things together — as if I was the same age as her — but now that she's at university there's a hurdle between us. I can't do what she's doing. And I hate it.

She interrupts my pity party.

"Do you remember when you were cast as Annie when you were little? Remember how it was a group of kids my age doing the musical, but you had to participate, 'cause we had to do it together? And you got cast as Annie over everyone in my grade?"

It's like she's read my mind. I have a flash of connection to her. I know she misses me, too. Weird how we miss each other but we're in the same room. "I remember."

"You remember how some of the other girls were mad, but you were so good at being Annie that in the end you won everyone over."

"Why are you being so nice?" I kid. "Aren't you too busy to head down memory lane with your little sister?"

"That's right, Car. I'm always too busy for you. That's why I'm home now and seeing if you want to hang out today."

I head over to give her a quick hug. "Instead, it's me who is too busy for you. Right now." I pull a goofy face. "Sorry. I have skating. But maybe when I get back, we could do something."

♥

I step onto the ice for my practice, and I know people are looking at me — I'm in the fishbowl, and they are watching me while they eat in the snack bar. I love this opportunity to perform. Love it. Skating is all about the lines you are creating with your body — how pretty can I make it look? I do stroking first, two rounds of Russian stroking — step on the ice, one step left, one step right, ending up on the short side of the ice. I go counterclockwise, take a few steps, then I do some crosscuts, walking-to-skating to get to the long side. I stretch out and do crossovers, heading left. I hold and pause, then do one crossover to the right, hold and pause. My mind and my body become one as I repeat continuous cross steps to make a shallow S pattern, then I do a U and start over.

every battle of a thousand miles starts with a single step
#figureskating #love ♥ ♥ ♥ ♥

I'm warm now, and my body is no longer fighting me. I need to warm up my edges next, and I work on my slalom — beginning with a two-footed, which I don't always do. But today I feel like everything is coming easily to me. I do a bunch of simple turns, thinking again of the people watching, then I do brackets, rockets and counters.

I think about the jump I want to do: my double axel. Shin shows up as I'm simulating the air position I'm going to need when I start jumping — two backspins in the center of the ice. He watches quietly. I'm too busy focusing to look up, but I picture his dark eyes upon me, weighing up what I need to work on, and it makes me want to work harder.

"Carley, hold," he says, as I finish my single axel.

I grit my teeth in frustration. I don't want to stop in this moment — I'm very square, and I'm perfect to jump. But I force myself to stop so I can listen to him.

By the time I get home, I'm stewing. All practice, Shin was on my case. Every step, every turn, every jump. *Urgh.* I feel like punching something. I slam into the kitchen, where my dad sits reading a John Grisham novel. He's at the wooden table by the windows, the one with the built-in bench, where all of us gather to eat family meals.

"I am so done with Shin," I say.

"Right," Dad replies. He hardly looks up.

"I mean it, Dad. I fired him today."

This is enough to get Dad's attention. He puts his book down.

"He went to the Olympics, Carley. And you fired him?"

I plop into a chair across from Dad and fold my arms across my chest. "Shin refused to let me fire him."

"What happened, exactly?"

"Just that. I told him, 'Shin, I'm done.' And he said, 'No.'"

Dad smiles broadly. "He's fired students. Good students, Carley. That's how it goes in skating."

"I know, Dad. I feel like screaming."

"But he won't accept being fired by you. Doesn't that mean something to you?"

"It means I'm super mad."

"It means that he really believes you can be good. That's why he pushes you."

I shove my fingers through my hair and pull a face. It's a goofy face — my mood is softening. "I'm sick of getting it wrong."

"You're not getting it wrong, Carley. The whole idea of skating is that you make it look effortless and easy, but it isn't."

"Kind of like Shin," I grumble. "He seems so quiet and mild, but he's a bear."

Dad grins at me and puts his hand over mine. "A bear you're going to have to apologize to."

I stick out my tongue. "Not now."

"No. Maybe now you'd like to have supper with your old dad — everyone else is out. Sound good?"

"Sounds great."

♥

The next morning, on my way to class, I see John. I call out to him, and as he turns to say *hi*, I swipe his hot chocolate and take a sip.

"I should start bringing you your own," he says good-naturedly.

The rush of other kids around us is loud, but for a moment everything stills. I suddenly see John, his dark eyes, his smile. I actually kissed him a couple of times when we were younger, way younger, but nothing has worked out between us. I remember when we were cast in the school play together as girlfriend and boyfriend and we held valentine hearts with the words *I love you* on them. A bolt of electricity arcs between us, and I feel my stomach quicken. I'm being so dumb right now. John and I are friends. We've been friends since we both started in a group together in the grade ten trip. It was hiking trip, and we must have hiked twelve miles. I have a great picture of me piggybacking on John, both of us laughing. So, John and I were flirting even then. That's what our friendship is — it doesn't mean anything more than that.

JOHN SERVINIS, Carley's friend

In November 2012 Carley had a skating friend from Finland who had moved to Toronto, and they became very close friends in a short amount of time. I met Carley's friend at a party, which somehow led to her getting in my car and me driving her as well as all my other friends home. When driving her home, she asked me, "So you are just best friends with Carley? I don't understand. Haven't you ever thought of dating her and having her as a girlfriend?" At the time I blew this aside, saying, "No way! That's Carley. She's my best friend. She would never date me. It would ruin our friendship."

♥

Carley thought it would be a smart idea to set me up with this girl. Carley's friend and I had a very short relationship that lasted three weeks.

RILEY ALLISON, Carley's sister

We would go over to visit Joni — our grandmother. She spoke Farsi. I was the oldest grandchild, and I had trouble with the Farsi word for *grandmother*. So, I used to say "Jon M," which sounds like a word in Farsi that means "my love, my sweet." My way of saying it turned into "Joni," which ended up being what we all called her.

Joni lived across the street from the Granite Club, where we skated, so during the summer we went all the time. Then in the fall I'd come home from university for a long weekend, and we would go over and watch *The Price Is Right* with Joni because Carley had a spare. Or Car would go before or after school with Mom, after Carley had swum at the pool in the building there. Joni's home was beautiful, a big apartment, with beautiful Persian decor — lots of rugs and gold. It was very grand.

Joni had surgery on her pancreas, and after that point she didn't really recover. As the fall went on, she was in bed a lot. Sometimes she'd get up and walk down the hallway. She loved it when we visited.

CARLEY

After school I head to visit Joni, my grandmother. Mom lets me in, and I kiss her on the cheek. She is busy cleaning out the fridge. Mom says, "People have been so generous with casseroles she can't eat them all."

"How is she?"

"She's in bed. Maybe we can get her to walk a little."

I walk through the gorgeous sitting room, over the rich rugs, and I run my hand on a golden figurine that I love. I remember when this apartment used to smell of these cutlets that we called "koobi" — meat, potatoes and onions, all panfried. They were frigging delicious. My mouth moistens as I remember, although now the place smells slightly antiseptic, and of cleaning products.

"Model Girl," my grandmother says from the bed. She is smaller, frailer, and this makes me slow my step. Just a little. I don't want her to see my expression. It's just hard because I remember my grandmother being so full of life all the time. Her dark hair is pulled back from her face, and her eyes are bright and full of life. Suddenly, I feel comforted. She is going to get better. I know she is.

She assesses me. "You know, I looked like you when I was young. I know you don't believe it." She adds in Farsi, "So pretty, so pretty."

The words sound something like *Khalie-ghashang,* and they are words she's used for me for my whole life — so I know what she means. I wish I could speak her native language. I wish I could connect to that part of her life and her history. She was born in Tehran. I can't even imagine what that would be like.

"But you're too thin, Carley Joon." Joon is her pet name for all of us; it means "my love."

"I'm eating just fine," I say. "Promise. I've been working out a lot to get into shape — I want to be able to do triples. And I'm going to record two songs for my audition to go to Berklee — imagine, me going to school there? It would be so amazing to study music and voice like that."

She smiles. "Ah, my Model Girl. Big dreams. You make me so proud."

love you and Papa more than anything.

KAT TSIOFAS, Carley's friend

I remember Carley was having some trouble with her skating. She wasn't landing some of her jumps that she had normally been able to do. Her skating coach, Shin, was getting on her case because he thought she was out of shape. Carley, being the competitive girl that she was, really took this to heart. I remember her saying that she was out of shape. She would note that she was getting out of breath just from going upstairs — this coming from the girl who had done the CN Tower climb in record time.

Carley and I were similar in the sense that we were both very hard on ourselves when it came to our sport. At first I just thought Carley was being hard on herself again. As her friends, we tried to support her, telling her there was no way she was out of shape and that she was one of the fittest people we knew. Then when things weren't getting better, Carley started with the doctor's visits. She was diagnosed with exercise-induced asthma. I think mentally this made Carley feel better. Now there was an actual reason that she was getting out of breath, and she thought this meant she could continue with her normal training schedule.

CARLEY

I went to the recording studio to record a few songs for my Berklee audition, and the recording engineer asked me if I could breathe quieter ... I didn't really know how to do that, because my breathing was always loud and that's just the way it was.

HOLLY DE JONGE, family friend

The family dog, Jack, would always sneak up to Carley's room and sleep by her side at night. It was almost like he knew first that something was wrong.

MAY ALLISON, Carley's mother

My mother, Joni, was in hospital for Christmas, but we were able to take her out for a night. I vividly remember forcing her out of the house, pushing her to go out. She so enjoyed being out. She sat in the car and looked out of the window at the Christmas lights. She loved it as we drove slowly through our neighborhood so she could see the lights. It was a big deal for her. Mark filled our yard with several blow-up toys and lights. The whole front lawn looked like Disneyland. She was very happy that night.

Joni was an amazing woman. I remember from her hospital bed she said to me, several times, "You make sure you find out what's going on with Carley. She's lost too much weight. You make sure to get it looked at."

Joni died on January 26, 2013.

CARLEY

My heart is breaking. But I'm not going to cry, no way. Our family arrives at the R. S. Kane Funeral Home, the same place we had Papa's — my grandfather's — funeral just two years ago.

Once we get inside there are pews as if it's a church; the place is all dark colors and lots of red. I think of my grandmother, her soft hands, the way she called me "Model Girl." My grandmother was so selfless. She was so kind. I make a promise to myself in that moment. If I can be kind to someone, I will. If I can do something to help someone, I will. If I can inspire someone, I will.

Sammy, my younger sister, leans into me, sobbing. I put my arm around her. I can start by being kinder to her. Uncle Glen finishes his speech, and it's time for me to sing with Ri. I'm trembling, but I won't cry. Not now. I have to do a good job for Joni. I have to smile.

This song is one that Ri and I wrote together, and during the chorus — *"Don't worry about us, we're good"* — my voice cracks. I'm struggling through the whole song with my breath. It must be heartbreak that is making it so hard to sing. I turn to smile at Ri as we finish our song; our voices fall silent, leaving a space for my fears to grow. In a few minutes I will sing alone, and I suddenly worry I won't be able to do it — my breathing is heavy, and my throat hurts. I just want to sit back and cry.

But I will sing my solo, and I will kill it for my grandmother.

LYNDSAY REDDICK, Carley's friend

Carley's grandmother passed away, and I remember going to her funeral, and my sister and I were both really concerned because Carley had dropped a lot of weight. I was more concerned about that than her breathing, because you couldn't really hear her breathing when she was just standing there talking.

She sang at the funeral, and then you could hear her difficulty in her breath when she sang. She had applied to Berklee College of Music around this time, and she recorded two songs for her audition. You could hear, when she was singing, the moments that she needed to take a breath. You could hear her labored breathing.

I remember we always used to Snapchat, and one day Carley said she was going for tests, and she sent me a Snap. She had all these probes all over her head and chest, and she was in a hospital bed in a hospital gown, being tested, and then she went home that night, but she couldn't breathe. She was having a lot of trouble breathing. So, her mom, May, rushed her back to the hospital.

CARLEY

My mom decided it was time to take me back to the doctor. They sent us to have a VO_2 max test. My results were above average, but that was expected because I was an athlete. So, it seemed like nothing was wrong. Finally, we were sent to see a respiratory therapist. He had me do a few different things, then he and my family doctor decided to put me on a five-day steroid medication.

The five days on the medication were the most alive and energetic I had been in over a year. I thought I was getting better at last. Once I got off that medication, things felt even worse. The respiratory therapist decided I needed to see an ENT (ear, nose and throat specialist). My appointment was made for a few weeks down the road. I went home that day and started choking on my lunch. My mom knew it was time to take me to the hospital. They diagnosed me with basically a hole in my lung. They told us to come back on Monday for a follow-up appointment in the pediatric ward. My mom was shocked that they were sending us home. I still could barely breathe. My mom stayed by my side for the weekend and slept right beside me at night. But I didn't sleep those three days. I felt like I was running a race, and I never reached the end and never felt any relief.

We went for my appointment Monday, and they admitted me to the hospital. I sounded like I had just run a marathon, and I was losing weight by the day. The ENT sent a camera down my throat to take a look inside.

His face turned white, and he left the room. I wasn't scared at that point. It was all happening too fast.

CHAPTER TWO

Enjoy those you love.

— Carley

February 4, the day my life changed

On February 4th, 2013, I was sitting in my hospital bed waiting for the results of the CT scan. We had no idea what to expect; as far as I was concerned, I had exercise-induced asthma. Within an hour or so my parents were having a pretty serious conversation with my doctor. At this time I was still pretty clueless as to what was going on. I was an elite athlete, I had a healthy diet, yet I was always short of breath, so we always thought I had asthma for sure. My parents looked pretty upset, and I saw a few tears running down my sister's face. Now I'm really curious, all I could see was their facial expressions through the glass door of my room. They came back in and no one really said anything to me. My dad just held my hand, and my mom kissed my forehead, and they said the doctors don't exactly know what it is yet. I knew that was only half the truth.

MARK ALLISON, Carley's dad

The doctors made it clear that something was really wrong. I think Carley could tell, but she wasn't crying. She was already looking at it like a fight, like something she could get through.

We were all being brave for one another. May and I were trying to understand what was happening, but everything was happening very quickly.

The doctors said Carley had to go in for surgery.

CARLEY'S BLOG

Day One — After Surgery

The next day, I was on a stretcher on my way to surgery. For a while I thought I was having surgery to remove the tumor, but my doctor came back with some shocking news. The tumor was too large to be removed right away. So, the game plan changed a bit, and the next thing I knew I was getting a tracheostomy.

It was all happening so fast, the next thing I knew I was lying on the operating table. I lay flat on my back with a towel rolled under my neck to give it leverage. They said they couldn't give me an anesthetic for the first part of surgery because my airway was so small, and the swelling could clog my airway. I was a bit scared, I mean who wouldn't be, and I was going to be awake while they cut a hole in my throat. But it had to be done, so I closed my eyes and tried to be as calm as possible.

I woke up very confused. I was hooked up to a few different machines, I had an ECG monitoring my heart, I had an IV giving me pain medication, I had a tube through my nose giving me food, and I had a tube connected to my neck giving my oxygen. I realized I wasn't going to be able to move much, but as long as I sat still, I knew I wouldn't be in too much pain.

The anesthesiologist came into my room the next day to ask me about the surgery. He had been testing a new drug, and he wanted to ask me how it affected me and if I remember anything from the surgery. I think it was safe to say I remember 99.9% of it. When I explained what I remembered about the surgery, he looked horrified, the drug was supposed to mix up my memory so I wouldn't be able to remember the surgery. My dad pulled out a piece of paper I had written on when I woke up, it read:

It was so scary yesterday
they started putting the tube down
while I was awake and I couldn't
breathe I felt like I was under water
they had to like hold my legs and head
down cause I was screaming I think.
I thought I was going to die.

The anesthesiologist joked, "Well, I guess we have to use a higher dosage next time." It gave us all a good laugh.

I realized after experiencing a tracheotomy operation with no anesthetic I could probably handle anything, but I had no idea what I had ahead of me.

RILEY ALLISON, Carley's sister

I didn't want to leave her room. It had all happened so fast — one day everything was normal, and then it was all hospital, and us trying to keep up. Carley was still able to make me laugh, even through all this. I don't think she was as scared as I was — it was happening to her, and we just had to watch. And we didn't really know then what was going on — the doctors really weren't sure, and they kept changing their minds about what they thought she had.

Carley's friends were all wanting to come and see her, and she was happy about that.

LYNDSAY REDDICK, Carley's friend

I went to the hospital the day after her first surgery. I didn't know what to expect. Carley was in the ICU — intensive care unit — and she couldn't talk yet. When I was told she was using a tube to breathe, I expected it to go down her throat through her mouth, but instead a small hole had been made in the front of her throat, and the tube had been inserted through that hole: an incision in her throat with the tube sticking out, with a breathing tube attached to that. I was obviously shocked to see her like that. Although I knew she'd had a surgery, before that moment I didn't really know what a tracheotomy was or what it meant. It was pretty shocking seeing her like that.

Carley was lying in bed, swallowed up by her blankets and surrounded by the beeping and buzzing of machines. The conversation I made seemed so mundane and meaningless. She was unable to really respond; her only means of communication were hand gestures and typing on her iPad, because she couldn't speak with the tube in her throat. I was scared to touch her; it seemed like any connection would be painful. She motioned for me to sit on the bed beside her, but I couldn't make out her figure beneath all the blankets and didn't know where to sit. The doctors weren't sure how long it would be until she could talk and if she would ever be able to sing or speak normally again with her trach in. But, although she couldn't talk, Carley was still trying to chat. On her iPad she was asking me how school was, and I was just trying to talk normally and tell her about my day and my friends, and then after she tried to suppress raking, excruciating coughs, she motioned for a button to be pushed. I

guess there was maybe an overproduction of mucus or something because her body was trying to heal the incision in her
throat. A nurse had to come in and clear the tube.

Carley caught my eye and mouthed, "Don't look. Turn
around."

It was all I could do not to cry then and there.

I turned away and stared blankly at the wall until the nurse
left. When I turned around and looked at Car, her eyes were
staring blankly ahead, refusing to meet mine, tears streaming
down her face.

♥

I have never in my life experienced anything more heartbreaking — to watch someone you love in pain and be unable
to help them. Once I left, I only made it to the elevator doors
before breaking down. I was so overtaken with confusion and
sadness. I couldn't understand why this had happened to her.

CARLEY'S BLOG

Day One continuation — My amazing sister Riley

My sister Riley has been my biggest support my entire life and no doubt my biggest support since I've been sick. My sister and I have a really special relationship, I'd say better than most sisters, and it has really showed in the past few days. Since I couldn't speak, sometimes I would mouth out words, my mom would sit there with a confused look on her face, but my sister always knew what I was trying to say. Riley said that for the first day most of my vocabulary consisted of "warm and fuzzies." My medication made me feel warm and I couldn't remember the name of my medication for the life of me, so I would just mouth out "warm and fuzzies," and my sister knew what it meant — that I wanted more meds!

Riley is probably one of the most amazing people I know. When she found out I was sick she came home instantly and spent the night in ICU with me. My parents would say, "Riley, go home and sleep and you can come back in the morning." But she insisted on staying with me. The night of my surgery my parents basically forced her to go home to sleep, so she went home, but she didn't relax. Riley and one of my best friends, Jill, were at my house making posters of my favorite quotes. The next day when I woke up they were all over my hospital room wall, it was incredible.

IF ANYONE CAN DO IT, IT'S YOU.

FEAR ABSOLUTELY NOTHING.

DREAM BIG.

♥

Day Two — ICU

I woke up today a little less comfortable than the night before but I was quickly distracted from that. I have 74 messages on my phone: clearly the word got out. I read through the messages and started to realize just how lucky I am. I have amazing family and friends, actually they are better than amazing, they are incredible. I don't know if I spent more than ten minutes with less than one person in my room today. The love I am getting from my friends and family is just the most amazing feeling, and I know it will keep me strong. There is no way this group of people is going to let me give up.

The trach was still sore and I was still unable to talk but I had started on my way to recovery. My parents always said to me, "If you're going to start a task, you better complete it and you better give it 100%," so I knew that's what I had to do.

When I signed the paper for my first CT scan, I made a promise that I was starting a task and I was going to give it 100%.

Every day from now, I start to get better.

MAY ALLISON, Carley's mother

She's hit with this, and there's hardly a tear. There's hardly a "Why did this happen to me?" She has always been able to hold it together. There was very little shock with her. And she's what's holding us together.

She was exceptionally strong.

CARLEY'S BLOG

Day Three — Back on my feet

Today I was finally able to get out of my bed. Although I wasn't allowed to go very far or be up for very long, it was still pretty exciting. ICU was a pretty closed off place from the rest of the hospital, and if you were a patient there, you were definitely not allowed to leave. So I started my little walk around the ICU, and it wasn't as easy as I thought it was going to be. I was sore and tired, and I quickly realized that it was much more comfortable in my bed. Quickly my focus changed, as I walked around the ICU, I could see into some of the other rooms. My jaw dropped at the condition of some of the patients; it was truly frightening. My mom noticed me looking, and she took me back to my room. For a few minutes I was in shock. I had heard about what ICU was like, but I'd never experienced it firsthand.

At this point my spirits were really down, I felt like I'd been on an emotional roller coaster ever since I got here. And this just happened to be a down moment. I don't think I really know how to deal with this yet. One moment, I'm laughing with my friends, and the next I'm wondering how serious things are. But I know that everything I'm feeling cannot even compare to how my parents are feeling now.

We wait patiently as another day went on and we had no results. My doctor had given my parents a few ideas as to what it might be, but I'm not so sure that was a good idea. I could see my dad pull out his laptop and start Googling all of the options, and I just watched his face turn white.

He came over to my bedside and said to me, "Carley, we are going to do whatever it takes to get you better. Whatever it takes." It was really breaking my heart to see my dad like this. He's always the strong one, always the rock. But not today. Today I could see him slowly falling apart.

♥

Day Four — The Diagnosis

Today I woke up in good spirits. I was feeling much better and I finally had that annoying feeding tube out. Just like every other day, my room was filled with visitors and the wall of cards was growing.

By mid-afternoon, my doctor came to deliver the news about what they found from the pathology. The pathology had determined that I had Malignant Melanoma inside the trachea. My doctor didn't seem very confident with what he was saying though: he said, "This is so rare that it's almost impossible that [you] have this type of cancer."

My doctor said that it could also be a Sarcoma Tumor, but

the pathology reported a Malignant Melanoma. After a little more conversation, my parents stepped out of my room with my doctor. To me it really didn't matter what type it was, because whatever it was I knew I was going to beat it.

A few hours later I was talking to my sister, and she says, "Hey, Numba Seven." For a second, I just burst out laughing because when I was on my medication, everything seemed to be funny. But after I was done laughing, I asked her what number seven was suppose to mean. She began to explain that if I really have Malignant Melanoma outside the trachea, I would be the seventh in the world to be diagnosed with this type of cancer. We kind of just joked about it, and changed the subject, but although it sounded cool to be seventh in the world, it was terrifying. I'd make light of it in front of my friends and family, but I couldn't help think about what comes along with rare things. Is it treatable? what kind of treatment would they do, chemo or radiation? Will it come back later in my life?

But I guess all that doesn't really matter anyways, like my dad said before, we will do whatever it takes.

MICHAEL NADEL, family friend

On February 4, 2013, Carley could barely breathe. She was rushed to the emergency department at North York General Hospital to undergo an emergency tracheotomy to create an airway. That's when the attending physicians discovered a two-inch, golf-ball-sized tumor that had disfigured her trachea, leaving Carley with a mere three-quarters of an inch of airway for her to breathe.

Originally, the tumor was misdiagnosed as a malignant melanoma of the trachea, and Carley was told she was one of seven people ever diagnosed with such a cancer, making the odds of contracting such a cancer approximately one in a billion. However, it became apparent that her type of cancer was even more obscure: a clear cell sarcoma of the trachea, which had only been diagnosed once before in the history of modern medicine, at Johns Hopkins Medical Center in Baltimore, Maryland. The odds of contracting such a cancer was about one in 3.5 billion, making it one of the rarest cancers ever diagnosed.

MARK ALLISON, Carley's dad

During grades ten and eleven Carley would have people over at the house, and her friends would come over. Callum, John O., John. I didn't differentiate between anybody. I met them all. But this was different.

This was when I really met John. We were in the hospital, and it was my night to stay with Carley. And John came and was not leaving.

Four hours went by. John was feeding Carley. His mom had made chicken with a mushroom cream sauce. I remember thinking, Who is this guy that's staying here so long? And that was my real introduction to John.

JOHN SERVINIS, Carley's friend

On Valentine's Day when I came to visit Carley at the hospital, I brought her a sock monkey that held a heart, which we had to sneak in as they didn't allow stuffed animals in the ICU. Carley's family and friends wanted pictures and everything to decorate her room with. Someone got Carley and me to be in a photo together, but as I went down to lean closer into Carley for the picture, I felt the urge just to kiss her on the cheek, and so I did.

when the days seem dark, remember people who love you

CARLEY'S BLOG

Day Five — The move out of ICU

I was really starting to feel better and get a hang of having a trach. They decided I really didn't need to be in the ICU anymore. I'm still seventeen, so they were going to move me to pediatrics, but I wasn't well enough just yet to go there, and the nurses were not very familiar with the tracheotomy. So I was moved to a room on the fourth floor that held three people. Luckily the room was empty and I was the only one being moved into it.

so incredibly lucky and grateful #friendsforever #fuckcancer

Even when I thought the wall of cards couldn't get any better, it did, and my family and friends moved it all piece by piece while I was sleeping.

♥

Day Six — My Girls

It was really nice to be out of ICU, but I really missed my nurse, Demara. She really made my experience in ICU as comfortable as possible, and always gave tons of support. Demara also acted as a friend, since I have moved out of ICU she has visited me almost every day after her twelve-hour shift in ICU. She's one of those people that are so passionate about what they do, and no doubt she always kept a smile on my face.

Another really great thing about being out of ICU is that my friends can finally come in more than pairs of two (although we broke that ICU rule a few too many times). During the second day in my new room a group of my best friends came to visit, and they came prepared. My friends didn't really do what the average hospital visit is generally like: walk in, say hello, ask how you're feeling, tell you to get better soon, and leave. My friends stayed for hours! But this day in particular they really raised the bar. They came in determined to not only keep me smiling, but also get me healthy again.

I lay flat in my bed while my friend Sydney painted my toenails, my friend Jill spoon fed me my dinner, and my friends Denzelle and Katherine kept me updated with everything going on at school.

my girls love you all so much ♥ ♥ ♥ ♥

I had no appetite, but my doctor said I had to force it. The moment Jill got wind of this news she was determined to fatten me up again. Jill definitely has some motherly instincts.

My mom stood at the door of my room watching the way friends cared for me, and it brought her to tears. My friends are truly incredible people.

♥

Day Seven — Realization

Today started the same as most days here in the hospital. Wake up, answer some messages on my phone, start my mango smoothie, and order breakfast. But shortly after breakfast the visitors started flowing in. I think it's safe to say I had more than fifty visitors throughout the entire day. I was overwhelmed with support and love, but one thing really stood out for me today. Today was the first time I really heard the word cancer being said openly. It kind of took me by surprise. My dad always referred to my tumor as a lump, and when people asked about my diagnosis my dad would mostly respond, "She has a lump in her throat." So I wasn't really used to hearing tumor or cancer. By this time most people were starting to find out bits and pieces about first pathology report results. I distinctly remember the first moment I heard someone refer to my condition as cancer. I almost felt a bit uncomfortable, as if it were a swear word or something. I looked around the room and saw a few more stunned faces: we had just never heard someone come out and say it. I knew it was going to happen sooner or later, but I was really hoping for later.

It was finally starting to feel real: I have cancer. But it's so different being the one with cancer, as opposed to being around a loved one with cancer. It all comes down to control. I have complete control of beating this, and of staying positive and healthy. My mom on the other hand feels like she has lost all the controls, and I know that's what scares her the most. I try to comfort her and tell her I'm strong and I'm going to be okay, but I know she just wishes she could make it disappear.

This quote was sent to me today from an amazing figure skater I got the honor of getting to know very well in 2011, Shizuka Arakawa: "God never gives us more than we can handle."

♥

Day Eight — Roommate?

My sister and I were enjoying the company of our two best friends from summer camp, Lyndsay and Jenny, when we noticed an unsettled lady being rolled into my room by stretcher. The emergency room was overflowing that night and I had two extra spots in my room. My sister, my friends and I watched as they moved the screaming middle-aged woman into my room. My nurse stood outside the room, speechless: she knew this wasn't appropriate. I soon found out this lady did not want to be at the hospital. Nurses were holding her down as they tried to get her settled into a bed, and every moment the nurse turned her head, the patient would try to escape.

I was sitting in my bed, pretty scared. I wasn't so sure what to do. All of this commotion was happening a few feet away from me.

Although I was scared I also felt bad for this woman. I didn't know why she was here, I didn't know her story. But from what I could see, she didn't want any help.

The head nurse on my floor got wind of this news and immediately came in to make some changes, and my mom and sister were already on the job. My room was supposed to be closed off because I'm still a pediatric patient, but clearly the head of room assignments was not aware of that. The woman started acting up, even more so than when she was brought into the room. My sister closed the curtain around my bed and came and sat beside me. Luckily the woman was only here for another hour or so until she was moved into a room of her own. My sister sat beside me and noticed I wasn't smiling. I was feeling extremely overwhelmed.

This is the first night I broke down. I knew it was going to happen sooner or later, and everything I have found out over the last few days was really starting to pile up. I just needed something to set me off. I guess it made sense for me to finally just cry it out. I lay in my bed, while my sister sat in a chair beside me. I asked her when I was going to be better, but she had no answer for me. No one really knew when all of this was going to be over, it's one of those things you can't exactly put a timeline on. All we can do right now is stay positive and hope for the best! I went to sleep thinking of this quote: "Once you choose hope, anything is possible." Christopher Reeve.

♥

Day Nine — News on the diagnosis, going home soon!

My doctor has decided that they want a closer look at my pathology report. They thought it would be best to send my results to Princess Margaret Hospital for further investigation because of the rarity of the situation. This also means that it will be another week until we get any more results. My mom and dad were pretty distressed that we didn't have any answers set in stone yet, as without answers I can't start treatment.

My nurse came into my room to clean my trach and said, "May, do you want to try this time?" (May is my mom.)

I looked at my mom with wide eyes, and then back at my nurse and said, "Mom doesn't know how to do it!"

My nurse began to explain that I would be going home in a few days and my mom would have to learn how to take care of me. I am pretty independent for someone my age. I like to do things myself but I guess I was going to have to let my mom take care of this one. The first time she touched it, I screamed. Not because it hurt, but because I thought it might. By the end of the day, Mom was really getting the hang of it and I was starting to get excited about coming home.

I also finally got to change out of my hospital gown! Our family friend Nancy and her two daughters Tasha and Lexi had brought me some really comfortable PJs, so I couldn't wait to take off the gown. Nancy and her daughters are more like family to us though. My sisters and I used to board our pony, Oreo, at their barn and ever since then we have grown so much closer. Nancy is truly an amazing woman, she was always like our mom away from home. I can't wait until I'm better and we can all go on a trail ride together just like old times.

MAY ALLISON, Carley's mother

The trach had an inner canula (tube) and outer tube. The inner tube had to be cleaned several times a day, but the outer tube only had to be changed every few weeks. Changing the outer tube meant taking the entire trach out and leaving Carley with a hole in her neck. It was a little more complicated than we were comfortable with, so whenever we were at the hospital for a visit, we would ask if they could do it for us. They told us we had to learn how to do it, but we always got somebody there to help us with it. I felt better when they did it.

Everything in our lives had changed, but Carley was, if anything, even stronger than before.

CARLEY'S BLOG

Day Ten — Missing my old day-to-day

My friends came in at lunch as usual, and caught me up on the latest news at school. And for the first time ever, I really missed my old day-to-day schedule, especially school and skating. It wasn't just the social side to school either; I really missed the feeling of accomplishment, and structure. My hospital days did not have much structure, and there wasn't a whole lot to accomplish other than eating my whole plate of food or going on a short walk. A normal weekday for me before I was sick would be packed from six a.m. to ten p.m.; days filled with the desire to improve myself and get closer to reaching my goals. Now, I lie in a bed for about 23½ hours of the day. It's really hard to adapt to such a drastic change, and feel like there is nothing I can do about it.

I have started to figure out that there are ways I will be getting that sense of accomplishment, and I will have goals to reach, it will just be in a different way than I had ever imagined. I'm going to be starting treatment at some point, and we will have checkpoints to see if the treatment is working. I guess those checkpoints will kind of be replacing skating competitions for a while. Like a skating competition I will need to be in the game physically and mentally prior to and during the specific date. From what I've heard and read about, half the battle of beating cancer is mental. I have learned how to prepare mentally for skating competitions, so I know that I will be able to give 150% mentally and physically to eliminate this tumor.

I know I can beat this; it's just a matter of time.

♥

Day Eleven — Going home!

I woke up to the sound of tape peeling off the wall, and I was pretty confused. Most nights before bed, I would have to take my medication in order to get a good night's sleep. So I would wake up pretty drowsy, which would explain why I was pretty discombobulated. I slowly opened my eyes and saw my mom and dad breaking a sweat. Knowing my parents, I assumed they were working out and doing laps around the hospital or something … I felt pretty embarrassed as I quickly realized that wasn't what was going on. They had taken so many trips up and down the stairs carrying toys and cards to the car that they were breaking a sweat. When they noticed that I was awake, they said, "You're going home!"

A feeling of relief rushed over my body as I sank into my bed and said, "Thank God that was the last night I had to sleep in this bed."

I got up, washed my face and changed into some new clothes my mom had brought for me. It was still a little difficult to get anything over my head, since the tracheostomy was still very sensitive, but I'm sure it will get easier as time goes on.

When I was leaving my room, the excitement to leave started to fade. It was like I had a little family here that I was leaving. The care that I got at the hospital was amazing, and it was pretty nerve-wracking to know that they won't be around 24/7. But I have this under control. Well, at least I think I do.

When I walked through my front door, the first thing I saw were my skates sitting outside my skating bag. I was immediately in tears again. I feel like certain things set me off, and seeing my skates was definitely one of them. I quickly pulled myself together, I didn't want my parents or my sisters to see my crying. I collected all my things one at a time and brought them up to my room, and if I thought the wall of cards in the hospital was crazy, it was nothing in comparison to the volume of love in my room.

JOHN SERVINIS, Carley's friend

As soon as Carley had been discharged out of the hospital, I started to visit her, bringing over movies. It was somewhere around February 20 that I brought over a movie for us to watch. I just wanted to be close to Carley, so I decided that we had to sit in the same La-Z-Boy chair. I soon kissed her neck and then slowly went to her lips. I have never been a person to be nervous about anything, but this was a time that I will always remember because I was trembling throughout my body.

While she was kissing me, I started to laugh. She gave me this distinct look that only she could make and said, "What's wrong?"

I replied, "Your trach tube is blowing on my neck and tickling me." This was the first moment I knew I had feelings for Carley that could not be suppressed.

CARLEY

I'm in my bedroom, but everything's changed. I'm listening to Taylor Swift. "Change." And I vow to myself that even though my life has changed, I'm going to regain control of it. I think about how I felt when I first arrived at the hospital and how quickly my world turned upside down. I look at the words on my wall: *Love, Hope, Dance, Dream.* And now the quotations from my friends that were on the ICU wall, especially "Never Give Up."

I'm going to be the person I know I can be, the person my grandmother saw when she saw me. I am not going to put doubts in my mind. And the first thing I'm going to do is get my singing voice back — I'm going to live the way I always lived before. Just even better.

I try to sing along to the song. Immediately, my voice breaks through the trach tube. It makes me want to scream. Not that I could probably scream very loudly right now. The scream would come out as a croak. I try again and again until it actually hurts.

One amazing thing that has come out of this so far is the blog — it was given to me as an assignment as I guess I can't really go to school for the moment. But I'm loving how people are responding to my words — how they are fighting this with me. I can't yet name the thing I'm fighting — I find it hard to let that word come to my mind. Not yet. That hurts even more than singing.

I read over the updates I've put on my blog and smile at the responses. I'm so excited that Dad's friend Michael has offered to help me get the word out there — he said he could be our media spokesperson and I laughed. Well, it probably didn't sound like a laugh through my trach! But he was serious. He said, "Carley, you have a story to share. You can make a difference and I can help you."

You got this, Carley, I say to myself.

Yes, I do. I need to stop feeling sorry for myself — this isn't me. I'm going to get out there and beat this thing. I reach my arms up and do a slow twirl in the middle of my room. Much as everyone was amazing at the hospital, I love being back in my own space. I imagine myself going on the ice and spinning, I tip my head back. And start to cough. I am dizzy and breathless. I sit on the edge of the bed. I hate to admit it, but I am too weak to skate.

Today, there's no way I could get onto the ice. Maybe tomorrow.

I make myself get back up. I don't want to give the doubts in my mind time to grow, and sitting around really isn't doing me any good. I head into my bathroom and put on some makeup — a soft-colored lipstick, a little blush. I pout at the mirror.

I got this. I do.

I post a happy photograph to Instagram. Someone pushes open my door.

"You're supposed to knock," I say as I come out of the bathroom, to see my little sister standing in the middle of my room. "What?"

"You look nice, that's all," she says.

"Thanks." I pull a goofy face at her. "Why are you in here?"

"It's just nice to have you back in your room."

"I bet you're just trying to borrow something."

She giggles. "No. I'm serious. I missed you."

"What?" I insist. "What is it you want?"

"Okay, okay. Your blue shirt. It would look good with these jeans, right?"

"The shirt you're wearing looks good with those jeans. But fine." I go into my impeccable closet and pull down the shirt she wants. "This better not be crumpled up on the floor of your room tomorrow."

"Promise. Thanks, Car. You're the best."

"Yeah, yeah. Now, get out of here."

She pauses at the door. "I did miss you. I am glad you're back."

I'm about to tell her that I missed her, too, but her phone rings, and she heads off to answer it. I glance at the sock monkey John gave me. My whole body thrills as if he's in the room with me. I remember what happened between us last night, and I smile — it is our secret. I press my lips together and follow Sammy out of the room. I make my way downstairs. I might not be able to sing. I might not be able to skate. I might be feeling just a bit sorry for myself right now.

But I can still eat a muffin and hang with my mom in the kitchen. For today that's okay. Tomorrow I will be better than this.

CHAPTER THREE

Happiness is found in the day-to-day.
It is found in the smile of someone who loves you.
— Carley

CARLEY

In Haliburton Highlands, at our family cottage, I cliff-jumped to prove I was just as good as my boy cousins, even if I was a bit scared. I pretended I was perfectly confident, and I jumped. And this is how I plan to deal with this little setback in my life. Cancer does scare me, but I'm going to be brave, pretend I'm perfectly confident and jump.

RILEY ALLISON, Carley's sister

After Carley's tracheotomy, the doctor told Carley that talking would be difficult. Then one day in the hospital Carley walked into the bathroom and needed something, so she yelled out. It was a Saturday at the hospital, and there were forty people around, and we all looked at one another. She could talk!

And in Carley's head if she could talk, she could sing.

I went back to school after Carley came home from the hospital. One day I was walking to my house from class, and Carley sent me a video. When I got back to my house, I watched it. My housemates saw me drop my phone. Because Carley was singing!

She was singing a song by One Direction, one she had learned to play on the piano, and her voice sounded great.

Instead of saying, "Hey, look, I can sing," Carley was asking if it sounded good. She wanted to see if she could *really* sing. In the songs she started making around that time, her voice sounded almost the same, other than her having to take deeper breaths and the trach making farting noises. If she could get a take where the trach didn't do anything, her voice was like her normal voice. It was unbelievable.

She already had videos up on YouTube from before her surgery. Lots of people had questions about her journey. I think Carley figured that if she just shared the video of her singing on YouTube, then people could see it and share her journey. And she thought that if it could help somebody else at some point, then she should share it.

A woman reached out after Carley posted the video and told

Carley that her son had been afraid to speak after his trach went in. He was five or six. After seeing the video, he wanted to speak again. His mother said she was in tears writing that to Carley. Even that email was enough for Carley to want to keep posting and sharing her story.

CARLEY'S BLOG

Singing with the Trach!
Posted on February 26, 2013

So, today I was playing around and figured out that with one of the caps I have for my trach, I could actually sing! Hope you like it!

VIDEO: Carley Allison — "More Than This" (Cover)
www.youtube.com/watch?v=zAhvUhEEq0A

♥

Baby Steps

I figure if I wear a scarf, I can go out and it will be like nothing is wrong, but I was definitely being a little too optimistic. My mom said to me, "Why don't we take it slow, maybe just go out and get a coffee, then come home?" I've never really been the kind of person to take baby steps. I responded with, "Let's go to Yorkdale!"

My mom bit her tongue and took me, my sister Riley and her best friend Natalie to Yorkdale.

I think I lasted about twenty minutes before I wanted to lie down. Once we went to my favorite store (Victoria's Secret), I was ready to leave. I looked around at my mom, Riley and Natalie and said, "Anywhere else you guys want to go?" but as expected they turned the question around to me.

i love you so much mom! You are incredible ♥ brunch together with my family. #bestmomever

I was exhausted but I didn't want them to know. I wanted to prove myself and show them that I was able to function perfectly normally. I responded saying, "Well, there's not really anywhere else I NEED to go."

And with that we were on our way out.

My mom asked me countless times if I was okay, and I just responded with a quiet yes. We both knew I wasn't okay. She could see me sweating through my wool headband, and coughing up a storm. Yet I wasn't going to admit it, and even though we both knew I was lying, we knew it was one step closer to me being able to say "I'm okay" and really mean it.

It was a lot harder than I thought it was going to be. It really put things in perspective for me. Walking around the mall should be a no brainer for the average person. But I'm not the average person, the average person doesn't have a trach hidden under their scarf, and a 5 cm tumor in their neck. I needed to accept that things are gradually going to get better, and just because I am out of the hospital doesn't mean I'm 100%. I'm going to have to learn to take things slowly, take baby steps.

MICHAEL NADEL, family friend

When Carley was released from hospital with her trach in her neck, only ten days after being diagnosed with a virtually unknown, life-threatening cancer, she turned to music for comfort. Music was a central pillar in Carley's life. She was an accomplished singer-songwriter, pianist and guitar player, with aspirations to be a professional recording artist. Carley had already produced several studio recordings of her original music, such as "Stronger Than That," and "I Loved You," or her cover of "Skinny Love," which can be found on Carley's YouTube channel.

What Carley did next was exceptional — she put herself WAY OUT in the universe by posting herself on YouTube singing One Direction's "More Than This" with trach and all, while skillfully accompanying herself on the piano.

Carley's video came to the attention of Selena Gomez, who promptly tweeted out words of encouragement and love to Carley and Selena's millions of Twitter followers.

Meanwhile, Carley's story was garnering the attention of the local media in Toronto and the national media across Canada. She had consented to sharing her story, and I was happy to help her bring it to the world. It wasn't long before Carley's story went international, with coverage by CNN, Huffington Post, Yahoo!, Associated Press and other news agencies across the world.

As a result of the media campaign and her blog, people from around the world learned of Carley's story and responded with thousands of emails of encouragement and thanks for helping them muster the strength and courage they needed to fight their own battles. It became evident that Carley was having a significant impact on others and had become an unofficial spokesperson for people facing adversity.

Messages between **CARLEY** and **SARAH FISHER**, Carley's friend

SARAH:

> 14.9 thousand people now know you're a singer thanks to Selena Gomez!!!!

CARLEY:

> OMG. I know! Crazy!!!

SARAH:

> If One Direction tweets you next, I'm requesting a shout out!!!!

CARLEY:

> OMG. One Direction would be AWESOME.

MARK ALLISON, Carley's dad

I was not interested in the media attention and preferred to deal with Carley's cancer in private. I was wrong to think that way, as I saw firsthand how well Carley dealt with the media and how the media shared her story. It made Carley feel like she was helping others, and I think that ended up being very therapeutic for her.

CARLEY'S BLOG

Grad trip out, Surgery in!
Posted on February 27, 2013

Today I spent the day at Princess Margaret, where I met with a team of doctors to develop a plan of action, and I was more than happy with what has been decided today. Although I had a CT scan less than a month ago, the surgeon that was going to be working with me decided he wanted to have a more recent scan. Before they did the CT, a scope was done to take a close look at the tumor. My surgeon's eyes widened as he looked down the scope and said, "This is much better than what is shown on her CT." My parents sighed in relief.

He informed us that I will have to go upstairs for my CT, then come back down to review it. The CT scan was just as uncomfortable as the first time, the injection tends to give me a major headache. Once that was done we headed to Starbucks to kill some time while they reviewed my new CT.

My surgeon came into the room and said, "Good news, we can remove it."

I had the biggest smile on my face. Apparently my first CT showed that my tumor was five centimeters, but now it shows a 3.7 cm tumor. I never thought in a million years that I would be ecstatic to hear that I had a 3.7 cm tumor in my neck, but I am. The timeline is looking a lot better now. Previous to today, I was being told that I won't be back to my regular self until late August. I refused to believe that, and I guess I was right to ignore it. Today I was told I should be done treatment by late May! I wanted to jump up and celebrate, but I was still in a little pain from the scope, so I stayed in my seat.

My surgeon began to explain what was going to happen during my surgery. It did not sound like it was going to be a simple job. We knew this from the start though — my case is extremely rare and not a simple fix. Regardless, they were going to take the tumor out, and after some time recovering, I will be strong again and ready to start radiation. As we were leaving, my dad pulled his phone out to put in the date for my surgery. He erased "Carley leaves for Grad Trip" and inserted "Carley's Surgery." Not really the March break I had planned, but it's what I got, so I gotta embrace it!

MARK ALLISON, Carley's dad

I remember deleting it in the calendar: *Carley leaves for Grad Trip*. And then writing in *Carley's Surgery*. Carley was disappointed, I think, but really she was focused on getting better. So she just shrugged it off. All of us knew it was the right thing for Carley.

CARLEY'S BLOG

7 days away
Posted on February 28, 2013

After my long day yesterday at Princess Margaret Hospital, I really started to digest the information. Yesterday I was just so happy to hear that they were going to surgically take the tumor out that nothing else said that day was going to upset me. But when I woke up today, I really started to think about it. Before today, I didn't know if I was ever going to even have surgery, let alone what the surgery entails. Yesterday, I was told that I was going to have a large incision along my collarbone so that they can access the entire tumor and lymph nodes around it. They also told me that they were going to have to remove my thyroid. The moment they said they are going to remove anything my ears perked up, but they assured me that I would just have to take a thyroid pill to replace it. As far as I was concerned the risks in this surgery didn't seem like such a big deal, until they mentioned my vocal cords. The doctors explained that there could be infected areas around the nerves close to my vocal cords, this means that there is a chance that my voice is going to change. I started to get a little worried. They said that the chance of a permanent change in my voice was very small, but I would most likely have a rasp in my voice for a few weeks. I was a little stunned to hear how complicated this surgery was going to be, but I should have expected that. I don't have the average case of Sarcoma. Regardless of what is technically going to be done during surgery, I know I have an amazing group of doctors, and they will do everything in their power to remove this tumor. I wanted to thank my Craniosacral therapist Janique Farand-Taylor. She moves my skull bones with gentle, subtle technique, to promote healing. I believe in her and her work, and I truly believe she is the reason my tumor is small enough to be surgically removed now. As opposed to February 4th, when I had my first CT scan and they said my tumor was too large for surgery. I have not been doing any treatment other than Janique's Craniosacral therapy, so I wanted to thank her for her amazing work, she is truly incredible. There aren't words to describe how thankful I am.

7 days till surgery.

♥

Allisdicks

Posted on February 28, 2013

2 Allisons plus 2 Reddicks = an Allisdick

I know that I have talked about how amazing my friends are before, but it's honestly the most incredible thing I have ever seen. My friends are some of the most extraordinary people in the world. I feel so lucky to have such caring friends, and for some reason today I was thinking about all the time they spent with me in the hospital. My room was generally a crowded place, but the one-on-one time I got to spend with my friends was always the best. One night nearing the end of my hospital time I had about eleven people in my room, including my friend Jill. Slowly throughout the night people started to leave but Jill stayed until every single person was gone. Finally, once it was just the two of us we walked downstairs to the cafeteria. We had small talk for about thirty seconds before she asked me, "So how are you really doing?"

I was immediately in tears. I was scared, and it was getting really hard to stay strong 24/7.

I looked up and saw tears running from Jill's eyes.

She said, "This kind of stuff doesn't happen in real life." We were both just silent for a bit.

I knew she was taking this really hard from Day 1, but you would never know, she is one of the strongest people I know. For the first few days after my tracheotomy I wasn't able to talk, so it was a shock when people visited again and I was talking. My closest friends from school came at lunch to visit me one day, and for my friend Sydney this was going to be the first time she heard me talk again. At the time, I didn't realize Sydney didn't know I could talk, so when I saw them coming into the room, I quickly said, "Hey."

Sydney burst into tears, but smiled at the same time. This girl has the biggest heart out of anyone I have ever known, and I don't know what I would do without her in my life.

Last night we got a pretty big snowfall so the roads were pretty messy, but that didn't stop my sister and my best friends from camp from coming all the way from Aurora. I guess that's what got me started on thinking about how amazing all my friends are, and how extremely lucky I am. The Reddicks (our friends from camp) have been family to my sister Riley and me ever since we met in 2006, and they have basically moved in since I got home. One of our traditions is Wing night, and even though I'm sick, there was no way we were going to miss out. I had been thinking about Wing night ever since I got the go ahead to eat after the tracheotomy, and it meant the world to me that the moment I said I was up for it everyone came over for our Wing night.

♥

My new normal
Posted on March 1, 2013

My life has literally flipped upside down in the last month. I went from being the girl that was never up to date with TV series or the latest movies, to the girl waiting impatiently for the next episode. I know that's not me, but it will be for the next little while, as I can't go to school for now. This morning I woke up at 11, I think that is probably the latest I have ever slept in my entire life. I started to notice the last few days I have been sleeping in pretty late but 11:00 am is just not okay. I actually woke up pretty irritable. I felt like I had wasted my whole morning. It's not like I really had much to do, but I wanted to get up and do something. Lying in bed all morning just didn't feel right.

I got up and went out for breakfast and a coffee with my dad. We got into my car, and I started to drive. I was pretty excited because I haven't driven in a while, but also because I got to spend one-on-one time with my dad. I have two other sisters, so in general it's not common that we often get one-on-one time with either my mom or dad. So I considered myself pretty lucky. My dad tends to always make me feel better about everything, and throughout the last month he has always been the most positive. I know that inside he's probably scared for me, but I would never know. He speaks about me with such confidence, and it just reassures me that I'm going to be okay.

When we got home from Starbucks, I went right back to the dining room where I had all my things set up. I have a lot of little projects on the go, things that I have always wanted to do but never had the time. I have my scrapbook on one side of the table, and all my old clothes and bathing suits on the other side ready for some alterations. I have always fixed up my old clothes, but now that I have the time it has definitely turned into an obsession, and now I'm begging my mom for a new sewing machine. I also spend a large portion of my day on the piano. Although it's still a strain to use my voice, playing is still that one thing that always makes me feel better.

The rest of my day normally consists of spending time with family and friends.

Today one of my best friends, Katherine, came over to spend some time with me. Kat has an extremely busy schedule since she is an elite volleyball player, yet she always makes time in her day to spend time with me. My friend Anastasia and her parents also stopped by tonight. I have been training with Anastasia since I was a little kid, but in the last year we both started training more primarily at other clubs. But we have definitely been able to stay close friends. Anastasia and her family are so kind and supportive that it's hard not to smile when you are in their presence.

Although my average day looks nothing like it used to, I'm doing everything I can to make it fulfilling. I've got the best group of family, friends and doctors behind me. I know I'll be back at it in no time, and my feet will be back where they belong: in my skates.

RILEY ALLISON, Carley's sister

Leading up to the operation to remove the tumor, Carley had to spend a lot of time at home. She had a lot of support, but it was still hard for her to be so inactive. She was the sort of person who loved to do stuff all the time, but now she had to rest. I don't remember anything specific about that time. I guess your brain just turns off when things are that traumatic. But her her diagnosis had changed everything between us. We became closer than we had ever been.

CARLEY'S BLOG

Pre-Operation
Posted on March 2, 2013

This morning my dad and I made our way down to Toronto General Hospital. 5:30 am was a pretty early morning for me, especially for me lately. My appointment was at seven, and we arrived just on time. We waited in a room, and we were told that I was going to be seeing a large variety of people within the next 2-3 hours. Within five minutes they were taking my blood.

Normally when they take my blood they use the little kid butterfly needle, but today they decided not to. I swear the needle was about ten times the size of the children's needle. But in the end, it was just a needle, and I had much bigger things to worry about. A few other nurses came in to do some tests and to take my vitals to make sure I was fit to go into surgery. We also talked to a nurse named Judith today for a very long time about what to expect for my stay in the hospital. Judith is a very good friend of my friend Leah's mom, who was also a former nurse at SickKids. It was really nice to be able to talk to a nurse who didn't only know me as the young girl with the rare case of cancer, but me as an athlete, and me as a person.

I should expect to be in the hospital for about two weeks, but this time I will be prepared. I know exactly what I'm going to need for the time I won't be able to talk, and the things I will need for entertainment. The day I was admitted to North York General, I had nothing with me other than my jacket. So at least this time I know what to expect.

The last person I saw was the anesthesiologist. She was one of the nicest, and funniest, women I have ever met in my entire life. She seemed so confident in my surgery and so sure everything was going to run smoothly, it was difficult to not smile around her. She went through the different procedures they would be accomplishing during my surgery. I just kept hearing … ostomy … ostomy … ostomy … ostomy.

I finally looked up and said, "How many different types of surgery am I going to have!"

She had a quick giggle and assured me that I had the best of the best surgeons working on me, and they have been doing this for a million years. She was definitely the most confident individual we have talked to about my case so far, and that was extremely comforting. She began to explain the drugs I would be taking and their effects, but I was just thankful I was going to be put asleep for this surgery.

Being awake for my tracheotomy will probably go down in the most uncomfortable moments of my life.

After we saw the anesthesiologist, we were ready to head to my next appointment. We got into the car and headed to

Janique's house for a craniosacral therapy session, where we would meet with my mom so my dad could head to work. My treatment was relaxing and calming as always, and it's always good to see Janique's puppy, Snow Pea. Finally my mom and I headed home. I looked at the clock and realized that I had done all that this morning and it wasn't even 12:30 p.m. It felt just like old times, exhausted by noon because I've already been up for six hours. Although I was tired, the feeling of familiarity was comforting.

My surgery is now six days away, I am both scared out of my mind and excited. I cannot wait for the day I get my CT scan results back to be able to say "I beat it." I know the surgery is just bringing me one step closer to that day.

♥

Mom ♥
Posted on March 3, 2013

Today for one of the first times my mom said I could go out with my friends, but I guess I didn't really understand her interpretation of "go out with my friends." My friends Carley M., Jill and Denzelle have planned for a long time that we would go shopping together for our grad trip. Although I'm sick now and can't go on the trip, we still all wanted to do this together. So I assumed I would go with them to the mall and come back with them. But my mom said no way. My mom had her mind set on coming. I was a little confused, I thought she had agreed to let me go. But my mom meant that, yes, I could go, but she would be coming, too.

I was pretty annoyed. I felt like I was back in Kindergarten when my mom found it hard to leave my side. I quickly realized that this was the only way I was going to be able to go, so I rolled my eyes and got into the car. When we got to the mall, I met with Denzelle, Jill and Carley M., and my mom did some of her own shopping. After about an hour I started to get pretty tired and my cough was getting strong.

That's the moment I was thankful my mom was there. I called her to ask her what store she was in.

She responded with, "Is it time to leave?"

I said, "Well, if you want to," but she knew exactly what I meant, even though I didn't want to admit it, I was tired and needed to go home.

Evidently, my mom is always right, and even though I thought she was being crazy and overprotective, she was right.

My mom has been the one primarily with me through this, she's basically turned into a nurse. And although we may be starting to get sick of each other, there are no words to explain how grateful I am to have her. She is working extremely hard to try and make things as easy as possible for everyone around her, and I sometimes don't give her the credit she deserves. She wakes up early in the morning to get a smoothie made for me, a freshly cooked breakfast and a cappuccino, not to mention that she still makes sure to keep my little sister's daily routine exactly the same. She also keeps up with things that need to get done at work, even though she's not in the office. I have no idea how she does it. To say she's a superwoman would be an understatement. Working mom, Olympian, amazing smoothie maker, and definitely the most loving woman on this earth. The amount she has gone through in the last month is just not fair. But she has been incredibly strong for me, and I can't thank her enough. After all, I wouldn't be here today if she hadn't taken me to emergency when she did. The surgeon said if she didn't take me when she did, I would have asphyxiated in my sleep. My mom saved me. And I love her so much.

MAY ALLISON, Carley's mom

We all wanted for surgery to be over and for everything to go back to normal. It was hard to wait. Carley had so many of her friends come over. And John was there, too. She had media interest, which she loved and which made us proud of her — she wanted to inspire others even as she was going through this. She was what was holding us together.

But I just wanted her to be back at school and skating and for, well, for the nightmare to stop.

the only time you should ever look back is to see how far you've come #tbt

CARLEY'S BLOG

2006 — Carley Elle Allison
Posted on March 3, 2013

Can't wait until I can skate again, starting the countdown! Three months to go!

Celine Dion sang "Power of the Dream" at the opening ceremonies for the 1996 Olympics (The Olympics my mom ran the marathon in), and it's the song that always gives me motivation. Can't wait until I can get back on the ice.

♥

My little Club Champ!
Posted on March 4, 2013

Today was definitely a long and exciting day! I spent breakfast with one of my friends who brought me amazing bacon pancakes! By lunchtime my mom, sister and I went downtown for an afternoon of shopping. We had just sat down in Starbucks when my mom got a call. CBC wanted to have an interview with me; to say the least I was pretty excited! For anyone interested in seeing it, it will be on the news sometime between 5:00 and 6:30 p.m. tomorrow night.

This weekend was not only an exciting weekend for me. My little sister Samantha is a pretty amazing little ski racer, and she has not had an easy season this year. Sammy is one of the biggest daredevils I know, so she always gives every race 100%. Unfortunately giving it your all racing down a hill at high speeds has it consequences. Sammy had a pretty rough patch in her season where she had a crash on her second run for a few races in a row. This was all around the time I got sick, she would always say to me, "Carley I really want to win for you."

I knew she was getting pretty discouraged, but this weekend she did what we all knew she had in her. She had two clean runs at the Club Championships and was the fastest girl on her team, winning the gold medal! Not to mention she also got the coach's award today at the awards ceremony! We are all so incredibly proud of her!

She's a pretty amazing little firecracker.

CARLEY, on Toronto Sun News, March 4, 2013

"I was pretty upset when I found I had a tumor. I just wanted the tumor taken out of me. I was really not happy with the idea of having a trach, but I've gotten really used to it. It's really not hard to handle, but obviously it would be best if the tumor was small enough to take out in the first place."

CARLEY'S BLOG

Chemotherapy before surgery?
Posted on March 6, 2013

Today was a pretty crazy and emotional day. I started my day off with an interview with City TV, and shortly after, I had my craniosacral therapy. During my therapy my mom got a call from my surgeon. They have done some further investigation and believe that it might be better for me to go through Chemotherapy before I have surgery. Essentially I was devastated. I couldn't believe that my surgery was going to be postponed to a month from now. I didn't understand why all of a sudden I was going to need chemo first. I thought I was having surgery in two days! I was definitely pretty confused.

My mom informed me that we were going to go pick up my dad and we would be on our way to SickKids to meet with a doctor to make the final decision. I was pretty upset when we got to SickKids but that sadness quickly changed. As I walked into the cancer patients' section at SickKids, I saw two children about six years old playing in the toy room. They seemed like normal, happy children, yet they were very sick. I suddenly stopped feeling bad for myself. I thought about how the parents of these extremely young kids feel. It really broke my heart to see so many children are affected by cancer, and that really made me more passionate to make a change.

We moved into a room where we would consult with the doctor. After a long discussion, I felt like we had gotten nowhere. I felt as though the pros and cons of both options were equal. I was starting to get a bit frustrated; I don't like not having a fixed plan. I have been preparing to have surgery on Thursday and it's hard for me to just go with the changes when I had my head set to go in on Thursday. I know the doctors have my best interests in mind, so I will do whatever they throw at me. And if Chemo is going to be the best option then Chemo it is! Whatever they can do to get me better and back to my normal life as soon as possible.

I wanted to thank everyone so much for all the support — it really means the world to me. You guys are the reason I'm able to stay so positive, and I can't thank you all enough! ♥

JOHN SERVINIS, Carley's boyfriend

I told her in February, "Okay. Look, I'm going to ask you to prom. I'm just giving you a heads-up, like, 'Don't worry, you don't have to worry about, like, getting a prom date' this and that." And she's, like, "Oh, really?" I'm, like, "Yeah, but I'm going to make it so it's going to be a surprise, and it's going to be in the most inconvenient way ever."

I planned to ask her to prom. My promposal consisted of the r, o and m being spelled outside her house in flowers, a balloon and candles respectively. However, the p was a laminated sheet of paper that I had frozen in a block of ice. I froze a Tupperware of water. I told her, "I'm going to make you work for it, just a little." After thirty minutes of microwaving, hitting it with shovels, stabbing it with knives and throwing it against the ground, she finally got to the sheet of paper. It was, like, horrible, but she said, "I wouldn't want it any other way." Then I took her outside to spell everything out.

One of the things we had was that I would always surprise her, no matter what.

Carley and I started to see each other more and more. My parents would even let me go visit her on school days every night of the week. We would mostly have our dates in her basement. They consisted of watching movies always and sometimes going out for dinner when she felt like it, as she was self-conscious about her trach.

Messages between **CARLEY** and **SARAH FISHER**, Carley's friend

SARAH:

Tell me everything!

CARLEY:

So I might kinda have a bf — not offish but still.

Guess!

SARAH:

OMGGGGGGGG! Servinis???????

Cause if not that kid loves you. So cute.

CARLEY:

Yes!

SARAH:

OMGGGGG. That's adorableeee. He's sooooo CUTEEEEE!

How did it happen?

CARLEY:

Like first time was about 3 weeks ago and I just pretended it was nothing lol, and I didn't tell anyone haha. He was over and like we always flirt and joke around and he was just kissing me on the cheek a lot and then he just kinda kissed me and was telling me that it's different with me and stuff.

SARAH:

What did you say. Awww. That's so cuteee ☺ He's actually the nicest human being lol

CARLEY:

He's legit amazing and my dad's like in love with him

SARAH:

So you've always sort of had a thing for each other

CARLEY:

Like he's been my best guy friend in forever. And he bought me flowers when he got back from the break.

SARAH:

;-) OMGGGGGG he's perfect. So sweet.

CARLEY:

But like I can tell he
really likes me.

SARAH:

I'm dying. That's
sooooooo perfect.

BRYAN AULD, Carley's high school principal

She's a fighter, she's an athlete and she's looking at this as if it's going to be another competition. I've been working in schools now for thirty years, and I've never had a student in this predicament. I've also never had a student I was this close to, and I would consider myself quite close to her in this situation. You just go this is, like, your kid. What do you do? What do you do to help the parents, and how do you? So you just do what you normally do, and you go and visit, and I'd go down a lot after school when she was down at the hospital, and bring tea and just talk and just make sure she was okay.

We missed her at the school. Her bravery and passion and her authority to keep everybody here on her side; and her friends were always wanting to be with her. There was very little that I saw of glum, of huge sadness really, really laid on, because she was always, like, "Don't worry, I'm going to get over this," even when the next hurdle came, and it came up. It was always going to be better, and that spirit was amazing — she just had a wonderful spirit.

CARLEY

I'm being as brave as I can. No. Braver. I'm telling myself I'm going to be okay. But right this moment, I feel not so brave. I'm sitting outside on the low wall in my front yard. No one knows I'm here — but in a few minutes John is going to show up, and we're going to watch a movie. Of everything that's been happening to me, knowing I'll be in his arms feels so good.

The air is chilled, although I feel that spring is coming. In the dark I can make out small buds at the ends of the lower branches. And there is a smell in the air — it's not a gloomy dark, filled with damp and swirling winds, like in the fall. It's a safer darkness, a darkness that promises good things, a darkness that holds me close.

But even in the embrace of the night, I feel the fear growing inside me. I'm going to lose my hair. I know it's not a big deal in the grand scheme of things — there are awful things happening in the world all the time ... wars and mass shootings, and people with nothing, no homes, no families, and kids with cancer who are really suffering. So, I know that I shouldn't care about my hair. But as I twirl a strand of it in my fingers and tug, I feel like something else is being taken away from me. And I can't figure out a way to take back control — I've tried so hard since I first went into the hospital to take back control. I sang with my trach in — even Selena Gomez heard me! And the surgery gave me control — I was counting down the days.

But my hair. It feels like it's being taken from me, and I can't work out how to own this, how to stop feeling sad and sorry about it. Cancer is a bitch. I still can't believe that's the word —

cancer. But I still don't look up and think, I have cancer. I hardly realized at the time, but it was my dad's fiftieth birthday when I was rushed to hospital, and we didn't get to celebrate on the day with him. Cancer took that from us as a family. But we're going to celebrate his next birthday. I'm going to have beaten this thing. It will be the best gift I can give him.

I rest my hands on my thighs. They are still thin, but I have gained a little weight. My hands feel solid and warm, almost like I'm holding myself up. Although really my family are holding me up — they have done so much. Riley has taken so much time off school. My mom and dad have had to take time off work, and they've lost so much sleep — when I think about what I'm going through, I realize it's nothing compared to what they are going through.

The night is quiet; there is a soft breeze, a promise through the leaves. A promise of the future that's coming. I force myself to stop thinking about my hair. I think, instead, about John — not hard to do. This cancer has taken things away from me, sure. But it has given me one thing. It has given me him.

CARLEY, on CTV, March 6, 2013

"We decided that I was going to be doing chemo, so I thought if my hair's going to start falling out, then I should just cut it off because right now it's healthy."

LYNDSAY REDDICK, Carley's friend

Carley started doing interviews almost immediately once she could talk again. The news picked up on her story, and how rare the cancer was, and that she was a singer who now couldn't sing. And then she started posting YouTube videos when she learned how to sing with her trach, and the media really responded to it, I guess, and then she decided one night — I was at her house; I think Jill and Denzelle were there, as well — and she said, "I'm going to cut off all my hair. I don't need it. I'm about to start chemo — someone should use it."

The news found out about it, and we went to her hair salon, and she cut off all her hair.

I was holding her hand while they cut her hair off, and I remember her being so brave, and we were joking about it, and I remember catching her eyes in the mirror, and she had tears in her eyes, because I think it was a moment where she had been so positive and hadn't really been thinking about it, and then she was watching someone cut off all her long blond hair, which she loved, and she was, like, Holy shit, this is happening. At that moment I was back in the ICU, struggling to hold back my own tears, thinking how selfish it was for me to cry, when she was the one experiencing the pain.

JILL HARRIS, Carley's friend

She made having her hair cut off seem liberating, even though she was probably scared.

CARLEY'S BLOG

12 Inches to Locks for Love!
Posted on March 6, 2013

Today I cut off all my hair so I could donate it to Locks for Love before I start losing it during Chemo. Some of my friends and family joined me in the salon to give me the support I definitely needed. Although it was pretty emotional to say goodbye to all my hair, I knew I was going to lose my hair either way, so why not cut it off when it's healthy so I can donate it.

♥

Friday's the day!
Posted on March 7, 2013

So according to the plan in place now, I am starting chemotherapy on Friday morning. I will be completing two rounds of chemo and then following up with a CT scan at the end of the month to reassess. Its going to be pretty difficult to go through the whole month and not know if the chemo is making a difference. But it's one of those things you just have to do, and have faith it is doing its job.

Its been pretty hard on my family, my mom especially.

Change in plans isn't something my mom likes. My mom likes to hear a plan of action, and have every date fall into place as planned. But this is going to be a bit different, we have to stay open-minded and easy going. If they say, "No surgery, we are doing chemo first," then chemo here I come. It's going to be a hard concept to get the hang of, but I'm sure as a family we can do it.

Friday is my first step to tackling this cancer, and I could not be more excited. I cannot wait to finally start feeling like I am fixing the problem and not just sitting around at home. I am confident that we have collectively made the right decision to start with chemo, and I will be starting my journey to recovery.

Friday's the day!

CHAPTER FOUR

It's life, and we have to enjoy it as it is.

— Carley

CARLEY'S BLOG

Day 1 Down
Posted on March 9, 2013

As most of you know today was my very first day of treatment. Chemotherapy was the drug of choice. I wasn't too fond of this idea at the beginning but my doctors assured me it was the right route. After seeing all the smiling faces in the day ward where I was today, thoughts about me were washed away. So many small children playing like it was any other day just with some toxic drug going in through an intravenous. They were my idols. It really goes to show how cancer is all a mind game and how just a smile can make it all better even for a little while.

Messages between **CARLEY** and **LYNDSAY REDDICK**, Carley's friend

LYNDSAY:

How's it going today girly?

CARLEY:

Meh. I'm already feeling it.
The screen is blurry.

LYNDSAY:

Oh no. Is it making you tired?

CARLEY'S BLOG

Chemo Day 2
Posted on March 10, 2013

So I can only type with one hand, so this blog may be a bit shorter! Today was my second round of chemo, and it was definitely better than the first one. Last night it was an extremely hard night. I was sent home from the hospital around 8 pm, only to return in two hours. I got home and went straight to my bed, a few minutes later I started to feel really nauseous. After some contemplation my parents decided I needed to go back to the hospital, with a barf bucket in my lap. Luckily they had kept a bed open for me just in case I needed it, and I definitely needed it. I was up and uncomfortable until about three in the morning, when they just had to give me a medication to force me to sleep and get me out of my misery. It's hard to explain how painful the side effects to my first round of chemo were, it wasn't like anything I had ever experienced before. My words to my dad were "I'd rather be dead than experience this pain." Just like Lance Armstrong said, "They have to kill you so you can live again."

I realize I'm not going to be feeling well during any session of chemotherapy, but I guess it's just doing its job.

MARK and MAY ALLISON, Carley's parents

MARK: There were two different kinds of chemo, and they were in three-week blocks. So, one of the chemos was five days long and then one of the chemos was only two days long. I guess the mandate was the nurse had to stay with you 24/7 because Carley had a trach. So, they didn't really want us to stay, because I don't think they had the staff, but we came home after the first chemo and she was so sick. Frighteningly sick. So we took her back to the hospital right away. I drove her back, and she was vomiting in the car, and we finally got back to the room. She was vomiting all night. I was up all night with her. I remember. I can still remember it till this day. She goes, "I never want to do this again. I can't do this. You can't make me do this." It was one of the moments where, although yes, she was very strong with a lot of things, she was so sick. But you know what? The next day they gave her more chemo.

And she said, "Okay."

MAY: It did get better. They sent us home with all these anti-nausea medications, but we had just spoken to our sister-in-law, who mentioned that there's a drug out there, a marijuana derivative, for anti-nausea.

MARK: It's called nabilone.

MAY: And it's —

MARK: It's a synthetic marijuana.

MAY: It's a synthetic marijuana, and she said they use it in the U.S. as an anti-nausea medication, but the good thing about nabilone is that, like marijuana, it makes you hungry. So, a cancer patient wants to eat. On a study they did with kids, the kids who didn't take the nabilone got thin during the process of chemo, whereas the ones who had the nabilone didn't get as thin, because they had an appetite. We asked for it, but it wasn't part of the protocol.

MARK: But we got it.

MAY: They gave it to us, and I think it was a savior for Carley because it gave her an appetite. It allowed her to eat, and she actually maintained her weight. She was already thin enough, right. So, she maintained her body weight a little bit during the chemo. It all just became our routine — we all started to live this new way with the hospital being at the center of it. Carley just accepted it; she just took it in her stride.

CARLEY'S BLOG

Finally out of bed!
Posted on March 16, 2013

So it's been exactly a week since I got my first dose of chemo and I definitely didn't know what to expect. Chemo was kind of one of those things I thought I would go, get the injection and come home and be perfectly fine. Little did I know. I was sent home after my first injection and I was back in the hospital within two hours violently ill. I was lucky the Hospital for Sick Children, which everyone calls SickKids, saved a room for me just in case I needed it. I stayed in the hospital for the next two days while I got the remaining dosages of my chemo, and they monitored my pain level. Even though it's been a full week it has only felt like a day or so. Sleeping through your days can get pretty confusing.

So, only one week after my first chemo things are starting to look forward. Although the chemo is making me feel sick and weak and nauseated, at least we know it's doing its job. I'd much rather push through the pain and know that it's really working, than just be guessing.

♥

Getting the hang of this
Posted on March 18, 2013

Last night was the kind of night that doesn't really seem to faze me anymore, just another late night trip to SickKids. Since I'm going through chemotherapy, the sign of a cold or flu is a little more of a red flag than it used to be. I started feeling a bit sick yesterday when I woke up but I thought I was just feeling crappy from my last round of chemo, but slowly during the day my temperature started creeping up. The doctors had told my mom that if my temperature goes over 38°C, I will need to go back to SickKids, so at 9:30 last night we made our way back down to SickKids for some antibiotics. It was a pretty long night, but you gotta do what you gotta do.

We met with the doctor to discuss the prescription, and she immediately looked at me and said, "You're new, right?"

I looked back at her with a smile on my face and said, "Yes."

She clearly had good relationships with the other families to have noticed so quickly that I was new. I've been at SickKids enough times now that I'm starting to see familiar faces every time I'm there, and it's definitely one of the most comforting things.

♥

Little note in my phone ♥
Posted on March 19, 2013

I was going through messages in my phone last night and I came across my notes. I have a new phone so I was kinda surprised to see that I had this extremely long note in my phone. I was pretty curious so I opened it and the page went on for days. I wanted to know who it was from so I quickly scrolled to the bottom, it read, "Love Syddy." Long story short, my friends Sydney, Chloe and Natasha had come over one of the days I was basically bed-ridden after chemo and just hung out while I slept and sat with me for the brief moments I would open my eyes. I only slightly remember seeing them that day but my parents and their note in my phone assured me they were here for about five hours. My friends continue to amaze me every day. They are all incredible individuals. It's been pretty hard the last week and a half, but it's times like these I know even when I'm feeling down I know no one is going to let me give up or ever give up on me.

Love you all ♥

♥

Back on the Ice!
Posted on March 20, 2013

This morning I decided that I was feeling well enough, and I wanted to try and get on the ice. I hadn't put all the numbers together and didn't realize that the last time I skated was January 30. That means I haven't skated in almost two months. I've been injured before so I have taken time off,

Remember this??? — The best big sis, when it rains it pours. There for me always xxxx

and learned to fight back, but I have never been off the ice for more than five weeks. Obviously this is different and I am going to be off for much longer than these two months, but it was so nice to be back on the ice today. Just the familiarity of being at the rink was just what I needed. Being at the rink was bittersweet though. It's hard to transition from being somewhere every day, to once in a blue moon. For a brief moment, when I was taking my skates off, a few tears fell from my eyes. I'm not too sure if it was because I was so happy to be there or because I miss it so much. But I think it's safe to say it was a bit of both.

Although I knew I definitely wasn't going to be able to train, or even do more than get my feet onto the ice, this is one step closer to getting back on the ice for good.

JOHN SERVINIS, Carley's boyfriend

I didn't read Carley's blog. I think that was a different part of her life that I just wanted to respect. So I wouldn't read it. I'd rather her just tell me.

She wrote the blog for two purposes: (1) for herself, as an outlet to express herself; and (2) to inspire those who were also battling cancer or could relate to her situation. The blog was like just good therapy for her to battle what she was going through. It wasn't only cancer she was fighting. It was a mental fight.

Messages between **CARLEY** and **LYNDSAY REDDICK**, Carley's friend

LYNDSAY:

> Good luck today girl!
> No matter the results your
> still gonna get through this
> and be a survivor at the end
> ♥

CARLEY:

> Thanks Lu ♥

LYNDSAY:

> Love ya :*

CARLEY:

> Love you ♥

LYNDSAY:

> Let me know the news okay!!

♥

CARLEY:

> This is fucked Lu

> It's like my decision

LYNDSAY:

What seriously?
Did the chemo work??

CARLEY:

No but they want to try more.

I'm fucking like bawling
my eyes out.

LYNDSAY:

Its okay Car, you can do
this. Life will never give you
anything your unable to
handle

Its gonna be hard but not
impossible

CARLEY:

☹

LYNDSAY:

Do you want to talk?
Im on lunch if you want.

CARLEY:

I can't right now ☹
with the doc

LYNDSAY:

Okay! Tell me if you want to meet! Your going to be a ok soon!

Allisdick adventures together

MAY, MARK, RILEY and SAMANTHA, Carley's family

MAY: I was always actually in a pretty good mood when we were going to the hospital, and you think that's kind of silly, but when we were engaged in doing something to make things better, it was such a good feeling. And we were used to it by then — it was just part of how things were. Waiting at home was very difficult, I found. The mornings we had chemo I'd get up and I'd say, "Let's get going." But chemo was horrific. For her. It just made her so sick. But I felt like we were doing something and so I was … I was happy to do it. After the first round she said, "No way. I'm not doing this. Not anymore." Remember how sick she got?

MARK: They also told us that they'd had very little success with chemotherapy in sarcomas. Very little. But our oncologist said, "Look, I think we should try. We'll do it once." So, it's a month … a couple of rounds of chemo. She said, "We'll do a CT scan, and if it hasn't shrunk by more than 10 percent, we'll go to surgery because we don't think chemo's going to work." They did the first round, and Carley got sick. She lost her hair. We went into their office and found out that the tumor had changed in its shape. It used to have sharp edges, and now it was smoother. But it hadn't really shrunk.

RILEY: The way the oncologist explained it was that the tumor wasn't, like, grasping on to her trach anymore.

MARK: The oncologist wanted to do more chemo. Carley just wanted to have surgery. She wanted this thing out of her, and I felt the same way. I said, "You told us that if it didn't shrink, we're not doing any more chemo." And the oncologist changed her tune. She mentioned that it was a rare cancer. I wanted to make sure we were doing the chemo for the right reasons — not just to get more data.

SAMANTHA: Because it was such a rare cancer in such a rare spot. The doctors seemed to be thinking, Oh, this is cool. No one's ever had this before.

MARK: As Carley was the second known person in the world to have a clear cell sarcoma in her trachea, we asked them, "How could this possibly happen?" The oncologist said, "It's just bad luck. There's nothing you could have done. It's not environmental. It's just bad luck. These cells have gone rogue."

Carley got really upset, and she was crying. We let her talk to the oncologist, who wanted to try another month of chemo. Carley agreed. And after that we did a CT scan, and it still hadn't shrunk, and the oncologist said, "We want to try another month."

JOHN SERVINIS, Carley's boyfriend

We were in the kitchen, and she was making me a salad. I looked on her shoulder. Her short hair was falling out. I didn't know what to do. I pretended to put my arm around her to rub the hair off before she noticed. And I hugged her from behind, giving her a kiss, too.

She asked, "What was that for?"

I said, "Thank you, for everything you are to me."

Messages between **CARLEY** and **SARAH FISHER**, Carley's friend

SARAH:

How are you feeling love?? ☺

CARLEY:

So much better!!!

SARAH:

Really?? :D good baby!!! Is it cuz your done your first round?

CARLEY:

Yeah but I start again in 1 week.

SARAH:

At least you feel good now!!

CARLEY:

Ya much better!!

SARAH:

Aw really? Are you done until the next round though?

CARLEY:

Yeah

SARAH:

That's good ☺ are you starting radiation then for your second round?

CARLEY:

Still chemo

SARAH:

I thought you were doing the surgery in a month?

CARLEY:

Yeah I am

SARAH:

Oh! When do they do radiation then?

CARLEY:

After surgery

SARAH:

Ohh okay I thought the radiation was guna shrink it

CARLEY:

it's different chemo and they have me on more meds haha

SARAH:

Is it stronger or less strong?

CARLEY:

Not as strong

♥

CARLEY:

I'm officially bald hahah

SARAH:

You look gorgeous no matter what!!

You probably rock it just as much as you rock the short hair!

CARLEY:

It's nasty

But I'm almost done

well I mean Im almost done this round haha

This could be my last round of chemo

Hopefully surgery will be in the middle of April

♥

SARAH:

How are you? Have
you heard anything yet??

CARLEY:

I'm alright, chemo again today

SARAH:

They're making you do
another round???

Do they know anything
yet with how it's doing??

CARLEY:

Yeah and it shrunk a bit

SARAH:

That's good! So what did
they say? How many more
rounds do you need?

CARLEY:

This is my last month

SARAH:

Yay!!! Are you happy?

CARLEY:

So happy I hate chemo hahaha

SARAH FISHER, Carley's friend

At one point, Carley was doing a week of chemo, a week off, a week of chemo, a week off, and in that stage, anytime she was on her chemo week it was harder; her energy was just much lower. But then when she'd be off her chemo week, Carley would get up and skate, she would sing, she was able to do a lot more. But when it was a chemo week, she would still push herself to, because that's her. Going through chemo — I think it's hard to do just about anything because of the amount of energy it sucks out of you.

One of my many favorite videos of Car is of her in the hospital (www.youtube.com/watch?v=ffF0Bd51R7o). She has an IV, and I don't know if it's a standard IV or if it's chemo, but she has one of those metal rods that you walk with, and it has wheels. And she jumped on it, and she was wheeling down the hallways of the hospital to the point where I believe the hospital actually put some sort of bracelet on her to know where she was because they thought she was gonna run away. But it was just Carley being herself; she was full-heartedly, genuinely laughing, thinking that it was so funny because she's got tubes in her and she's running through hallways, laughing. It's such a beautiful video of her.

Like I said, I think with chemo she would always push herself and want so badly to do everything, because that's the kind of person she was. She always was; she wanted to do things all the time. Like, sitting in bed isn't something she wants to do. She wants to be around friends, family. Make people laugh. Have fun. Smile, laugh. She just wanted to … she just loved life so much, and she loved doing things. She was so great at everything she did; she was a busy girl — she was always so busy. So for her to be just stuck in bed and not be able to do things sometimes was just very hard for her, I think. 'Cause she was watching all her friends being able to do all this stuff. And that I think was difficult. So difficult for any human — if you can imagine everyone you love being able to do everything you want to do. Everything a teenager should be able to do. And when she began chemo, specifically, I think that's when everything just became more challenging for her to be able to do. We would make plans, and she would try so hard, because she wanted to fight it so badly, to be able to get up and do things, but sometimes it just wasn't ... it just wasn't a good day for her.

CARLEY'S BLOG

Hanging out at SickKids
Posted on March 22, 2013

This morning my mom and I woke up at six and headed down to SickKids for my second round of chemo. When we got here I checked in and had some blood work done, and I have to say, it was the least painful needle I've ever had, so the day was off to a good start. I'm going to be here for five days of chemo, so it was time for me to get a PICC line. A PICC [peripherally inserted central catheter] line is a device that is connected to a more central line than an IV in my hand. Until this morning I wasn't aware that a PICC line was such a procedure. When the nurse was explaining what was going to happen, I looked at her with my jaw dropped. I said, "Are you kidding me?" but it has to be done so I have to suck it up.

After I got the freezing on my arm done, my mom and I were just sitting waiting for me to go in when the nurse came out and informed us that there was an emergency and my PICC line would be postponed for a few hours. So, with a frozen arm, my mom and I went down to the cafeteria for some lunch, and that's where I've been ever since. The waiting is draining but I'm still happy that I'm feeling well, because I know after I get my chemo I won't be feeling great for a few days.

♥

Chemo Day 2
Posted on March 24, 2013

Day 2 Chemo complete! I am so incredibly happy because this time around, I'm not feeling too sick. This is a much different experience to the last time I had chemo, but I'm not complaining! Things have been going pretty well here at SickKids. My friends came today to keep me company so I've been occupied all day. It's been pretty hard to sit in bed all day so I've been going for lots of walks. Since I had been skating for a few days before I came back here, I started to get the feeling of exercising every day back, but now that I'm in the hospital it's impossible to exercise and it's driving me crazy. But it's only four more days! Then I will be back home and able to get my feet back on the ice.

Mentally, it's hard because I just want to skate and I just want to get back to my normal life, but I have to be patient and patience is definitely something I need to learn. Although it's hard and I wish I could just wake up tomorrow and have this all be a bad dream, it's reality and I have to face it.

I may not be there yet, but I'm closer than I was yesterday.

♥

Chemo Day 3

Posted on March 25, 2013

Today I met another patient at SickKids, who is also my age and has a similar type of cancer. He also has a type of Sarcoma tumor. It was really refreshing to meet someone who is my age and going through the same thing. He was diagnosed in September, so he's a lot more familiar with the effects of chemo and with things around the hospital. It's been really nice to have someone tell me what I'm headed for. Not to mention that he's a super nice guy, and he definitely has a good head on his shoulders. I want to congratulate him on almost finishing his fourteenth and last round of chemo! Michael, you're almost free!

My hair has finally started to fall out so today my dad and I shaved our heads together! Love you so much, Daddy.

♥

Going Home!

Posted on March 27, 2013

Just sitting in my bed waiting for the doctor to come in and give us the go ahead. This round of chemo has been much easier on me physically, and with the exception of yesterday, I have felt pretty good. The next two weeks will be spent at home while we let the chemo do its job. On April 2nd, I am scheduled to have my CT scan, and the appointment with my doctor and surgeon will be a few days after. After this appointment we will decide if I am going to move forward with another month of chemo, or if I will go into surgery right away. Whichever option it may be, I know it will be made in my best interests, so I just have to let the doctors decide the new game plan!

Hopefully this time around I will go home not feeling so sick, and I can get back into a bit of a schedule before my next appointment. But I just have to be patient and see how things go!

♥

Moving forward
Posted on March 30, 2013

Unsure of what is to come next, I'm back home recovering from a round of chemo. This has been much better this time around, and I'm really starting to feel better, just curious as to what the game plan is now. But for now I'm just taking it day by day. Maybe I'll try and skate by the beginning of next week. I've learned that I need to listen to my body and slow it down when I'm getting tired. Fighting cancer isn't exactly the same as training. Sometimes I just need to take a step back and rest. But I'm getting stronger every day!

♥

Happy Easter!
Posted on March 31, 2013

Today my family and I went out for brunch for Easter morning. It's nice to know, even though I'm sick, that some things don't change. It was really fun to be out with my family, but it was also exhausting. I knew that I wasn't going to last that long, and I definitely had a well-deserved nap when I got home. I noticed today that leaving the house is getting a bit harder as the days go on. The only thing I had to worry about before was hiding the trach.

Now, I have to make sure my PICC line is tied up, my trach is covered and my bald head is covered. It's quite the process now. It's frustrating at times, thinking I'm forgetting something every time I leave the house, but it's what I have to do for now.

Every day is getting better, but it's a slow process, and I just have to be patient.

On another note, I am getting back on the ice tomorrow! Wish me luck!

♥

Crazy few days

Posted on April 3, 2013

The last few days have been quite insane. I was really starting to feel better the other day, then I woke up in the middle of the night Sunday in extreme pain. I had my white blood cell shot the day after I finished chemo, and generally it makes you feel pretty under the weather, but this was different. I got up and I could barely feel my arms and legs. I had no idea what was going on. I called my mom and dad into my room because I didn't know what to do. After Tylenol had no effect, we made the decision to take another middle of the night trip to SickKids. I think one emergency visit to SickKids between chemo therapies is becoming a tradition of mine.

We got to SickKids and they prescribed me some medication to take the pain away. The production of white blood cells in my bone marrow was giving me pain. So now today I'm starting to get my strength back and get out of bed. Well, I had to get out of bed because I had a CT scan at 10 this morning. So my mom, dad and I got up and headed down to Toronto Western Hospital, then to SickKids for some blood work. Everything went well so we were on our way home in no time.

Every time I walk into SickKids it's a bit different, because every time I go I meet more and more people and build more relationships with the staff. I know the hospital isn't really the place you want to walk in and be welcomed by name or hear things like "We missed you!" but it's definitely better than being a stranger or the new kid.

RILEY ALLISON, Carley's sister

Carley had people at the hospital who loved her — the other kids and the staff. It was just the sort of person she was. I guess we all were part of that community, and it was always fricking amazing to see when someone else got better, and we saw that coming for Carley.

CARLEY'S BLOG

What's Next
Posted on April 6, 2013

It's definitely not easy waking up every day not knowing what my life is going to be like for the next few months. I tried to imagine the two different options, Surgery or More Chemo then Surgery.

In my head, the best outcome of our meeting on Tuesday would be surgery. But I know that's not what I should be hoping for. If the chemo is working well, I will continue with chemo for another two months, and then go into surgery. Continuing with chemo would mean I recover two months later than I would have without it, but the tumor would be smaller for surgery. So there are some positives and negatives to both, but technically it is better if the chemo is working and I can continue with it.

Although it's hard not knowing what's next, I have really been enjoying the last few days because I have been feeling so good. I'm also excited for tomorrow!

We are having some of our friends over and a few of us are going to do the full head shave! Pretty excited, but also pretty nervous to finally have a fully bald head. I never imagined I would be shaving my head at seventeen, but it's an adventure, gotta embrace it.

LYNDSAY REDDICK, Carley's friend

Through chemo, Carley talked a lot just about being frustrated that she couldn't skate, and she couldn't sing, and she was tired, and she would get really puffy from the treatment — like, she would swell up a lot — and she just didn't feel like herself, and you get chemo brain. So, she just wasn't nearly as on as she was used to being, but I found that she really kept her humor through it. She obviously had her moments where she was exhausted and just needed to sleep, but once she was awake she was usually in pretty good spirits throughout the whole thing.

We had an event — a head-shaving party. Well, it wasn't so much a party. It was more that she wanted her friends there while it happened. She wanted her support system there with her while she cut the rest of her hair off, and I can't remember when this happened, but Riley was in university, and all her friends decided to have a head-shaving party, and so her dad, Mark, and her cousin Jeff said, "If you're shaving, if you're losing your hair when you have chemo, we're shaving our heads, too." And then all her older sister Riley's friends were, like, "We're shaving our heads, too, if Carley has to lose her hair." So we all ended up at Carley's; there were probably twenty-five or thirty of us in the house and backyard, and Carley got to shave everyone's head, and then she was bald.

SARAH FISHER, Carley's friend

It was a wonderful day. To see all these people come together for one person they all love, they want to show support for — it was wonderful.

CARLEY'S BLOG

Baldies
Posted on April 7, 2013

my friends and family made today so much fun
#fuckcancer

I wanted to say a huge thanks to everyone who made yesterday so amazing! We had such a great day and I was so overwhelmed with all the support!

Ten of our friends shaved their heads with me yesterday. The support is amazing, and I definitely wasn't expecting for so many other people to actually shave their heads. I am incredibly thankful to have these amazing people in my life. Also a big thanks to the best big sister in the world for organizing all of this. Love you, Ri!

just my best work of art

Special thanks to Daina Marsh for letting me steal her hat from her for a few months.

"When it's hard to look back, and you're scared to look ahead, you can look beside you and your friends will be there." Anonymous.

CHAPTER FIVE

Keep trying, because next time
you might succeed.
— Carley

JOHN SERVINIS, Carley's boyfriend

Carley asked me, "John, why are you with me?"

I answered, "Because you are something like no other to me."

She said, "How are we going to do this? I'm losing my hair, I'm going to be ugly. How will this work for you?"

I said, "You are so beautiful it won't even matter. I just always look into your big blue eyes and just smile because you make me so happy."

MAY and RILEY ALLISON, Carley's mom and sister

MAY: We purchased Carley a prom dress when she had the trach in. So, before any chemo, we went downtown and we bought her this very pretty dress. It was a big deal. Like, we hadn't done that for Riley.

RILEY: Dad picked my prom dress. I liked my prom dress, but because Carley was going through treatment, we wanted to do something special. So, Mom, Carley and I went to Holt Renfrew. We went to the second floor, where they have amazing dresses. Carley didn't think there was anything small enough to fit her. The dress that she found was silver, off the shoulder, a gorgeous, gorgeous dress. It was designer — Laundry by Shelli Segal. In the change room, which was lovely — I'd never been to a dress store like this — Carley stood on the pedestal, and this wonderful woman was helping us. The dress was four hundred dollars, which was very expensive, but as it was during her cancer fight, none of us cared. A Persian woman was also shopping, talking in Farsi, and she didn't realize that Mom could understand. This woman was trying on a dress and a pair of Louboutin shoes, and she couldn't decide how high the heel was going to be — 2¾ in., 3⅓ in., 4 in., 4¾ in. Mom was translating for us, and we were laughing a little at this ridiculous conversation about the heels. And then Carley was in the dress. She had a beautiful figure, and she looked amazing. It was never a question of whether the dress was going to look good on Carley, more if she was going to like the dress. She seemed unsure for a moment, but both Mom and I could tell — she really did love it.

MICHAEL NADEL, family friend

The Allison family received an email from MLSE — Maple Leafs Sports and Entertainment — management indicating that Joffrey Lupul, an ice hockey player for the Toronto Maple Leafs, had requested that Carley Allison sing the national anthem at the next Leafs home game. It was a very timely invitation, since the upcoming game was the last game of the regular season, a marquee match televised to millions of viewers on *Hockey Night in Canada,* with the Toronto Maple Leafs squaring off against their archrivals, the Montreal Canadiens. It was also the first time in nine years that the Leafs would enter the postseason Stanley Cup playoffs. A lot of excitement surrounded the game and the prospect of Carley singing the national anthem.

However, Carley was scheduled for her next round of chemotherapy that week, and the family knew that Carley would be in no position to sing the anthem. Further, it was clear that the family had no interest in postponing Carley's treatment, even if just for a week. It was evident that time was of the essence, since Carley's rare cancer had gone undetected for over a year, and due to the nature of Carley's cancer, each day was precious in order to learn more, experiment and try to find the right therapies to combat Carley's virtually unknown clear cell sarcoma.

CARLEY'S BLOG

Thank you Granite Club!
Posted on April 8, 2013

On Saturday the Granite Club Figure Skating section had a fundraiser in my name to raise money for SickKids hospital! I wish I could have been there to see everything, but I heard it was a great success. I wanted to take this opportunity to thank everyone at the Granite. I have been skating at the Granite Club since I was six years old and everyone at the Granite is like family to me. You guys are all amazing and I don't know what I would do without all of you.

♥

Chemotherapy Round 3
Posted on April 9, 2013

Today, I had a meeting with my parents and medical oncologist. We met to talk about continuing with chemotherapy or going into surgery. After a long confusing discussion, we have decided to go ahead with one more month of chemotherapy. The tumor has not, per se, shrunk in size but there has been a change in the texture of the tumor on the side touching my thyroid. This led my oncologist to believe that the chemo is having an effect and it would be best for us to continue with another month-long cycle. At first I was very upset with this decision; I wanted to have surgery and get on with my life. But I realized that by making the tumor as small as possible before surgery, it gives me a better chance of a full recovery. And although I am yet again set back another month, I'm confident that this is the right decision for me in the long run.

MARK ALLISON, Carley's dad

They kept saying more chemo, and then this will be the last round. She had lost her grad trip and all her friends got to go, and then we kept thinking the chemo would be over. And it was hard to know what the right thing to do was, and we wanted it to stop. But the doctors kept saying, "This will be the last round," and we just had to go with it. And we were grateful to Mike Nadel for all the media stuff that she got to do — it gave her something to do, and it felt like she was a star.

CARLEY'S BLOG

Just give me a reason (Cover)
April 9, 2013

New cover with the trach!

VIDEO: Just give me a reason (Cover) By Carley Allison
www.youtube.com/watch?v=f7IqTsCT8YE

♥

Almost done Chemotherapy round 3!
Posted on April 11, 2013

I started my two-day round of chemo yesterday, and I am feeling much better than I did last month after having this type of chemotherapy, so that is definitely a positive! Surprisingly these last two days have gone by really fast and I have already had my dose of chemo today. So depending on how I'm feeling, I could be on my way home tonight. But I know what I'm in for, for the next week. I will be getting my white blood cell shot tomorrow, so I know that will hit me in a day or so.

For now, things are going okay, and I will try my best to keep everyone updated this week!

"There will be a light at the end of the tunnel. I'm just not sure when we will find it." Anonymous.

♥

Awesome day at Kiss 92.5 Monday!
Posted on April 12, 2013

Just a day before I had to come back into chemotherapy I spent the afternoon down at Kiss 92.5, which Michael Nadel organized, and it was one of the best afternoons I have ever had. It was instantly like I was in a room with a couple friends showing me how they do their job. Before I was going to go on air with them Cash started to show me how a couple things work. I was blown away with how much work their guys have to do when they're not on the air. Although they have lots of work between times on the air, they are extremely entertaining the moment they are back on their air. I honestly can't remember the last time my cheeks hurt from laughing so much. Cash and Adam were both so welcoming and two of the nicest and funniest guys I have ever met in my entire life, and I am so thankful to have had the opportunity to meet them and be on their show!

♥

Chemo round 3 complete!
Posted on April 16, 2013

XO "It doesn't have to be easy, just possible." Bethany Hamilton, Soul Surfer.

Today I woke up definitely not feeling 100% myself. I wasn't in a good mood, and I was still feeling some of the effect from the chemo and WBC shot. I finished my third round of chemo last Thursday so I thought today would be the day I start feeling better again. I was a little disappointed when I woke up still feeling nauseous.

Feeling sick aside, I realized something today, I've already made it through more than two months since I was diagnosed and three rounds of chemo. So after feeling pretty upset this morning, I started to figure that if I've already been through two months, it'll just get easier from here.

My life has for sure done a 360 in the last two months, but I'm almost halfway there! And who knows, I may only have one more round of chemo to complete! Running on the chemo home stretch!

♥

Leafs Game!
Posted on April 19, 2013

Thanks so much to SickKids for sending me and my dad to the Leafs game last night! I didn't get to sing, but I can't believe I got to meet Joffrey Lupul and Andy Frost — he's the public address announcer for the Maple Leafs!

♥

Chemo round 4 starts tomorrow!
Posted on April 23, 2013

Today is my last day before my next (and could be last) round of chemo so I'm trying to get everything done before I go back, knowing I'm not going to feel great when I get home. This round is much longer than my last, but from previous experiences, it doesn't make me feel as bad as the two-day round. Obviously I wish I didn't have to go back, but I'm really excited to get this over with and be done with chemo for the rest of my life. After this round I will be having another CT scan and we will decide if I need another month of chemo, or if I will go into an operation. I am not sure what to expect but I can only hope that the chemo is doing its job.

♥

Quick midnight visit to SickKids
Posted on May 2, 2013

Last night before bed, my mom and I were just going through the routine of flushing my PICC line (the central line in my arm). Every night before we flush the line, we need to check for blood return. My mom was checking for the blood return and we were having a bit of a problem. It kinda freaked me out when I looked down and there was no blood coming through my line. I started thinking of all the worst possibilities, could I have an infection in my line? Could there be a blood clot in my line? We knew that we had to get to the bottom of this, and nothing is more fun than going to SickKids in the middle of the night! So we called our family friend to make sure going down was the right thing to do, and we hopped into the car and headed down.

We walked into emergency and they took me in right away and flushed out the line. I had a small blood clot in the entrance to my line. Within thirty minutes we were on our way home. Cranky and tired, my mom and I fell asleep within minutes of being home. But at least we could sleep knowing my line was clear and nothing was seriously wrong.

♥

Tired of being sick
Posted on May 6, 2013

These last few days have not been a piece of cake. Friday night my family and I went out for dinner and a movie. Halfway through the movie I realized that I wasn't really feeling well. When we got home, I went straight to bed. Little did I know that I was going to be up all night. About an hour later I woke up sweating and in extreme pain. I hadn't taken any medication yet so I pulled myself out of my bed and walked downstairs to find some medication. I first took my temperature because I knew that if I had a high fever we would have to take another trip to SickKids. In general, I have a low temperature, and the thermometer only read about 37°C so I decided I was good to take my medication. The thirty minutes it took for the medication to kick in felt like hours, but it did its job and I went back to sleep for a few hours.

I woke up the next morning feeling equally as bad as in the middle of the night, if not worse. I didn't really under-stand why: I had finished my last round of chemotherapy on Monday so I should be feeling good by this point. But whatever it was I had to deal with it. I spent all day Saturday in bed hoping I would feel well enough to attend the Skate Canada COS Ice Show that night. I checked the clock every minute as it got closer to the time I was supposed to leave the house for the show. When the time came, I still wasn't able to leave my bed. My mom got her things and went to the show to receive their donation [to the Princess Margaret Cancer Foundation] on my behalf. I was extremely upset that I couldn't be there to watch the show and thank Skate Canada for the donation but I was not in shape to leave the house yet.

I woke up Sunday morning feeling mildly better. I realized that I had caught a cold, and catching a cold when your immunities are so low isn't fun. It's more like a cold on steroids. All I can do is rest and wait till I start to feel better. It's been pretty hard to just sit in bed these last few days, knowing that I could be back in the hospital for more chemo or surgery within a week or so. I like to spend as much time doing the things I love in between hospital stays, and getting a cold feels like a bit of a setback. It makes me think, "When is this all going to be over? When am I going to be able to get back to just being myself?" It's not a familiar feeling waking up and having nothing to do, nothing to accomplish. It's been long enough now that I've almost forgotten what feeling normal and healthy feels like. And I know the day I feel normal again will be one of the best days of my life.

Although this isn't something I would have wished upon myself or anyone else, it has taught me things I would have never learned if I hadn't gone through this. In the past if a family member or friend wasn't feeling good or just had a cold and we had somewhere to be, normally I would have just said something like "maybe take an Advil, and you'll feel better soon," or "take a cold shower." I don't think I will ever say that again to anyone. Before I was diagnosed I had never been so sick that I couldn't walk or be self-sufficient, but now I know how it feels, and if someone tells me they don't feel good, my response would be more like "There's the couch. Here's some water. Do you want me to sit with you?"

Not that I wouldn't have done things like that before, but it has become so clear to me now that you never know how bad someone actually feels. Tomorrow I will have a meeting with my oncologist to discuss what the plan will be. This time I'm nervous but I know whatever happens I will have the amazing support of my friends and family.

CARLEY

When they told me I was going to lose my hair, I said, "Bring on the razor!" And through the rounds of chemo so far, I have been trying to hold it together. But they have just told me that I won't be having my surgery before my prom. Another round, maybe two, of chemo, instead. I mean, who gets to wear a trach for their prom party? Let me put my hand up, because it's me! This is what my treatment looks like, and I'm starting to realize we're nowhere near done:

- Emergency tracheotomy surgery
- PICC line insertion
- A million rounds of chemotherapy
- Tracheal surgery, hopefully one day to get this trach out
- Something else????
- And more????
- And then what???

I just want it all to be over. But now I feel even worse for complaining. It's not like I haven't seen all the kids in SickKids — I'm hardly the only one dealing with this. But this list of treatment plans isn't what I was hoping to be making. I wanted to be making a list like this:

- Land the triple
- Make a scrapbook of the photos of my grade twelve grad trip (the one I didn't get to go on)

- Have the best-ever prom with my girlfriends and my amazing boyfriend, wearing my gorgeous off-the-shoulder dress. Which I can't now because my trach will show if I wear it
- Skate and work all summer
- Take John to our family cottage
- Be the best I can be
- Grow stronger every day

At least cancer can't take the last two things on my list from me. And once this surgery is over, then I will take John to the cottage. Or maybe I should just take him beforehand — perhaps for Lobsterfest. Now, that would be something.

But first, I have to sort out a dress that hides my trach. I really, really don't want to be showing it off for prom, dealing with the "sympathetic" glances and the questions. No way. An idea sparks in my mind. I think the thing for me to do is design my own dress. I will still have my other prom dress, the one I bought with Mom and Riley, for another special day. A day when I am not sick anymore.

It won't be long now.

MAY and RILEY ALLISON, Carley's mom and sister

MAY: So, Carley had this beautiful prom dress with one shoulder, and it was gorgeous. But we bought that prom dress on the premise that she was having surgery. This is before the whole chemo option happened. We thought that she wasn't going to have the trach in. Then it became apparent that she was going to have the trach for prom, and so, we needed to find a dress with a collar. Right now, they're like a dime a dozen — dresses with collars — but at that point in time there weren't any dresses with collars. We looked and looked, and we thought about adding a collar, and finally we found someone to make a dress for us very quickly, in a week, and we went out and chose the material. And it just so happened the dressmaker, a lovely lady, had been through thyroid cancer herself. She and Carley designed the dress, and the lady made Carley a beautiful dress with a collar.

RILEY: It had a little sleeve pullover. She had a PICC line in to administer the chemo, and they couldn't take out the line. They wanted to keep it in for surgery. So, Carley had it in at the time. She carried this little cuff that went over top of it. It was cute.

MAY: These things, too, all required maintenance. Like the PICC line — you'd have to flush it every night.

RILEY: It was nasty.

MAY: Every night, yeah. Although they trained us to do it, every time we went in for chemo we asked them to do it.

JOHN SERVINIS, Carley's boyfriend

She came to school so I could take her out for lunch. She made me so nervous that day; it was the day I asked her to be my girlfriend. Officially. I blurted it out in the car. She said yes as I was getting out of the car and shutting the car door. I didn't want to hear her answer if she said no — I knew it would crush my heart.

I walked away looking down with a smile on my face, and once I got into the school, I told our friends Pouyan, Callum and Denzelle that I finally asked her.

CARLEY'S BLOG

Some Things Never Change
Posted on May 11, 2013

Practicing some skating moves off the ice. I think I'm missing skating a bit too much these days. It's pretty hard to break a tradition.

Tomorrow (Saturday) is the Granite Club fun Championships that I have competed in since I was a little kid. The only events I was signed up for were a father/daughter dance, and similar pairs with my sister Riley. Competing in pairs with my sister is something we always both look forward to: from picking the song, arguing over the choreography, shopping for costumes, somehow we always pull it together. This year Riley and I were planning on doing a Bollywood-themed performance. But unfortunately I am still in the hospital this year for the competition.

Good luck to all the Granite Girls! Have an amazing fun day!!

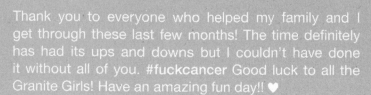

Thank you to everyone who helped my family and I get through these last few months! The time definitely has had its ups and downs but I couldn't have done it without all of you. #fuckcancer Good luck to all the Granite Girls! Have an amazing fun day!! ♥

RILEY ALLISON, Carley's sister

At the beginning of that year, Carley and I had said we were going to do a Bollywood-themed skating program. We already had the costume and the music, and the day of the event was something that we used to describe as the best day other than Christmas. Skating was so regimented with the practices and the choreography. But club championships — an interclub competition — was always just a really fun day. We had won the last four programs, so we were pretty excited about the whole day. We worked on choreography at the hospital, which was ridiculous. And Carley said that if the club championships day fell in a week between chemos, then she would do it. But the club championships fell the day after chemo.

We actually went. We didn't skate, but we went to watch. Car was pretty drugged up. And she was a bit embarrassed about her trach and being so skinny, but we sneaked her into the music room so she could watch the other girls.

Those are some of my favorite memories. She and I always talked about a comeback and how we would do it again.

CARLEY'S BLOG

May Two-Four Long Weekend
Posted on May 23, 2013

Lobster weekend. Even in the worst times, my cotty makes everything right #onthegull

This past weekend my family and I went to our cottage in Minden, ON. This was the first time I've been away from home since I got sick (excluding nights at the hospital of course). I was a bit nervous to leave home to begin with because I have been fighting a cold for a while but knew being at the cottage would make me feel better. We got to my cottage around 6:30 p.m. Friday and as per usual I went right to the dock. Normally I would jump right into the water, but the water is still a bit cold, and I think if I jumped in with my trach I would drown anyways.

So I sat at the end of my dock and watched the sunset with my feet in the water. I was quickly reminded why I say my cottage is my favorite place in the world. I was instantly feeling better.

Finished my LAST round of chemo! Lobster weekend #ninjaturtles #superheroes

Every year on the May long weekend, we have a big lobster dinner with the rest of our family, who also have cottages on Gull Lake. And every year we have a theme; this year it was Superheroes. We had a bit of a costume dilemma but we put some great Ninja Turtle costumes together last minute!

♥

Finished my LAST round of chemo!
Posted on May 28, 2013

This morning I finished my sixth and final round of chemotherapy, and I could not be more excited.

> Step 1. Tracheotomy **Complete
> Step 2. Chemotherapy **Complete
> Step 3. Surgery

Some days go by where I question if any progress is being made. But after days like today, I understand that things are moving in the right direction. I figure if I got through three months of chemotherapy, the rest will be a piece of cake.

Getting closer to the finish line every day!

RILEY ALLISON, Carley's sister

Carley and all her friends were excited about prom. Carley was feeling good. Carley and I went to a place at Don Mills shopping center called Murale, to get her makeup done. We'd been there before, and every time we went, Carley chose Bobbi Brown makeup and Tamara was the Bobbi Brown rep. But Tamara hadn't seen Carley since before the cancer diagnosis, so Tamara got really emotional. She kept welling up while doing Carley's makeup, but she did a great job — Carley looked beautiful.

My best friends ♥ my dad, and my amazing mom. I love you guys!

He's a pretty special guy.

Pre-pre-prom was at our house, in our backyard, and Carley had eight girls over: Jill, Denzelle, Katherine, Chloe, Anna, Carley M., Sydney and Gaby. Most of them were already ready. The idea of pre-pre-prom is to take lots of pictures with all your girls. Some of our other friends came, too, like Lyndsay, Megan, Sarah and Marissa. We gave them champagne and stood around outside, taking lots of pictures — it was a warm, sunny day. I think pre-pre-prom is the best part of the whole prom. That and pre-prom.

Pre-prom was at a friend's house on Lake Ontario. The place was stunning. There were many decks and gorgeous views, and the food was catered. Carley and John met up, and I took lots of pictures. Carley struggled with the boutonniere white rose that she had to pin on John. She didn't want to stab him.

JOHN SERVINIS, Carley's boyfriend

I went to Tiffany. I was going to get Carley a bracelet, and it was a hundred dollars or so, and then my dad asked, "John, how long do you think you're going to be with her? Do you really like her?"

I said, "Yeah. I really do. I can see myself with her for the rest of my life."

And then he said, "Okay." So then he took us over to a necklace. It had a C on it. We bought that for her. I always wear it now. I don't take it off — I can't even remember the last time I took it off.

I met Carley for pre-prom. I pulled out the little turquoise box, and she said, "I hate you so much." She added, "I didn't want any of this. You shouldn't have given me this. What are you doing? Don't even give me this."

I said, "Carley, I already bought it for you, and there's no one else who has a name that starts with C, so it's yours."

She smiled and let me put the necklace on, and she said again, "I hate you so much."

Prom was downtown. Inside the building, the lights were dimmed and everything was decorated in white. It was *Casino Royale*–themed, the James Bond look. Carley looked beautiful.

BRYAN AULD, Carley's high school principal

I remember Carley arriving at prom — she got off the bus, and she looked fantastic in her silver dress. More than that, she looked like a regular kid. I could see that was important to her — she smiled, and then avoided catching my eye after that. She didn't want to hang out with her teachers. She wanted to have fun. She was happy being a regular teenager that night. She wasn't thinking about cancer, and I was happy to see that she was enjoying herself.

DENZELLE HUNTER, Carley's friend

There was a big buildup to prom, and then prom itself was fast — it was all over at midnight, and then our after-prom ended up being at someone's house. And so we all went back to my house, and it was, like, very uneventful. It was just "prom's over." It came and went like that. Carley and I thought that was funny. All this buildup, and then it was over.

CARLEY

I touch my necklace from John and smile — I love it so much. And I love that I'm starting to feel so much better. It's been a few days since I finished my chemo. I went out on my walk this morning like I normally would, but I was feeling a lot better and stronger today. I decided that today I would try and jog for a bit, and it made me feel great. Being able to do a bit of running again really put me in good spirits. I know I need to be as healthy as possible going into surgery at the end of the month, so I might as well start now. After I went for my run, I decided to sing, and that's where I am now. I sit by the piano and fool around with a song I've been thinking about. I only have a few lines at the moment. I let my voice take on my lyrics; it's almost as if I'm enjoying my voice with the trach. It's different singing with the trach in. Okay. I don't enjoy it. Obviously, I can't wait to get the trach out. But it's sort of fun to fool around with my trach voice. I sing some possible lyrics for a song I've been working on:

> *"When I'm alone, sometimes I dream of how it used to be*
> *before I was tested on how strong I'd be.*
> *For one day, I woke up to a new reality.*
> *I start to think, is it worth it, putting up with pain? The*
> *never-ending unknown what the next day was going*
> *to bring for me.*
> *There came a day I found out just how serious things could*
> *be ..."*

I think I hear Mom and Sammy in the kitchen. I jump up. I'm still not sure where this song is going, so I'm happy to leave it for a bit. I'm excited about getting through this next step. Surgery. One thing I've realized is that my experience has been identical to a 400-meter race. As a previous 400-meter runner, I've learned a few things about the 400-meter race.

The race itself is a sprint, but unlike the 100-meter or 200-meter sprints, the 400-meter sprint takes patience. Though my situation this year has prevented me from participating in track and field, I've had a 400-meter race of my own.

The first 100 meters you start out strong, giving yourself that adrenaline rush as you power off the starting blocks. My first 100 meters was the original tracheotomy. Without anesthetic, I lay on the operating table and put on a brave face. This was a different kind of strong, though; I couldn't just push myself physically to give myself a good start to this journey. I had to be strong mentally to begin the battle to beat this.

At the 200-meter mark of the race you have to keep your pace and keep your focus. The second 100 meters is normally the least focused on by the crowd, as the start and finish of the race excites most people. The second 100 meters is where each athlete needs to find the strength inside to keep going strong. Chemotherapy was my 200-meter mark. It wasn't anything exciting like a surgery, but it was a time in which I knew I needed to push myself and keep the pace strong.

When you hit 300 meters you know you're almost there, and now it's time for you to pick up the pace. As you come around the corner, you're in sight of the finish line, and you know it's the most important time of the race. The most important time of my race is my surgery to remove the tumor. Although it's frightening, I can see the end, and that's what I need to focus on.

The last 100 meters you have to give it your all and give everything you have left. Push yourself to your limits, because you know you're almost there. Physically and mentally you're shot, and you don't know how much longer your legs will hold you. The six weeks of radiation will be my final 100 meters. I'll be mentally and physically exhausted from the previous five months of treatment, but I'll see the finish line, and I'll have to give it everything I've got.

Then, finally, I will have beaten cancer.

CHAPTER SIX

Scars are reminders of the
life you have lived.
— Carley

CARLEY

Earlier this year, on February 4, my life changed, and I am
so much stronger because of it. But right now, I am afraid.
I smile at the nurse, though, the way I smiled at my family
when I said goodbye just now. I will keep smiling, no matter
how hard this is, no matter how scary. There is the *beep-beep*
of machines, there is the smell of the hospital and there is the
fear — fear that this time the anesthetic won't work, like last
time. Fear that I will have every cell in my body in pain and
be unable to scream.

I push away the fear. I push out the smell. I push out the
sounds. In my mind, I am on the dock at the cottage, the water
icy cold around my feet — my feet are dipped in, and ripples
circle away as I wiggle my toes. Soon, I will jump in; soon, I
will leap.

But first, this surgery. And I will do it smiling. If it kills
me. ;-)

MICHAEL NADEL, family friend

After several grueling rounds of chemotherapy, Dr. Patrick Gullane, of the Princess Margaret Hospital, felt that the size and texture of Carley's tumor had changed enough to facilitate surgery. In early July, Carley's trachea was bisected and the affected portion — approximately two inches — was removed. The two ends of the trachea were reconnected, and the incision where the tracheotomy was performed was closed. Carley's postsurgical treatment included radiation therapy to irradiate any residual cancer cells.

CARLEY'S BLOG

Success in The OR
Posted on July 2, 2013

Hi Carley Lovers,

Guest blogger here, Riley, Carley's big sister ♥

I have the most wonderful news to share with everyone who has been supporting and following her story every day! So for those of you who don't know, Carley underwent a 4-5 hour surgery to remove the cancerous tumor in her trachea. Now we all knew Carley would just fly through this surgery, but hearing it from the surgeon's mouth was one million times better. At approximately 12:15, the doctor came out while I wasn't in the room. I slowly walked into the room noticing my mother's head in her hands. Terrified at what I didn't know, I instantly stopped in my tracks. My dad noticed my face and quickly said, "She's clear, they got it all out, the surgery went better than anyone could have expected!"

Immediately my mother, my dad and I were in tears in a group hug. The best news I have honestly ever heard in my entire nineteen years on this planet! My baby sister and best friend might I add, was going to be fine! She was going to be fine! Carley will be under for a few days and just a little out of it so you will probably hear back from me soon with Carley Updates. But for now I am going to go kiss my little sister and put her jewelry back on (the one thing she asked for).

xoxo ♥

JOHN SERVINIS, Carley's boyfriend

Carley had her surgery done, and I brought her a giant toy panda. Except, I went to the wrong hospital. I went to Princess Margaret, but she was at Toronto General, so I had to walk through the rain. It wasn't raining that much, but I still had to walk through the rain with a six-foot-tall panda. And this was when Carley didn't want me to see her. But she couldn't get mad at me because I got her a six-foot-tall panda. It was a really, like, love-hate relationship there, because she hated that I went against everything she said but loved that I got her the panda and surprised her with it, as I just showed up.

She was very angry, though, because she wanted to look nice for me always, but sometimes you can't always look nice. This was the day I could barely recognize her after her surgery, but I still remember being able to recognize her solely through her big bright-blue eyes that would always bring a smile to my face.

Messages between **CARLEY** and **SARAH FISHER**, Carley's friend

SARAH:

> CONGRATS ON GOING
> HOME BABYYY!!!!
> How do you feel??
> Can you talk??
> Me and Alex and Megs
> wanted to visit you! ☹
> but we can just come
> over now. Lol

CARLEY:

> Hiiiiiii I'm good!
> I still can't talk ☹

SARAH:

> Aw really?? Till how long?

CARLEY:

> I have a thing that acts
> as a cast for my trachea
> inside my trachea and it
> goes right through my
> vocal chords. I get it
> out in like 10 days so
> after that I can talk

SARAH:

> Is it uncomfortable?

CARLEY:

Ya like I can barely eat anything

I've lost 6 pounds ☹

CARLEY'S BLOG

8 Days since Surgery!
Posted on July 11, 2013

It's been eight days since the big operation and I am feeling great! Doctors said that everything is healing perfectly and quicker than they expected. I don't think I have yet wrapped my head around the fact that I am now cancer free! February 4th feels just like yesterday, and now I can say I am cancer free. It has been a bumpy road these past five months and I know I still have a bit of a road ahead of me but the worst is over, and the cancer is gone! It feels amazing to say, "I HAD cancer."

This experience as an inpatient at the hospital has been a bit different than all the others. At SickKids I was among other kids with cancer going through chemotherapy. At North York General (where the trach was put in), I was in a single room at the end of the hallway and I rarely saw other patients. Here and when I'm at Toronto General I am in a ward for head and neck patients. And I have to say, if I still had my trach, I would fit in perfectly. From what I can see, over 50% of the patients on this floor have tracheotomies, something I didn't think was so common. Although everyone's situation is a bit different, everyone on the floor has had a similar surgery and they are all so supportive. It is amazing how positive everyone is, and how determined they are to get healthy again.

It's hard not to be positive in an environment like this, and we have the staff at TGH 6B to thank for that. They are all a little family and I'm proud to be a part of it.

On another note, on July 16, there is a SickKids benefit at Mount Pleasant and Davisville from 3-7 pm called Concert for Carley! Anyone and everyone is welcome!

♥

2 days to go!
Posted on July 15, 2013

In two days, I will finally be getting the last tube out of my neck! I have had a tube in my trachea that acts as a stent since my surgery on July 2nd and it will be removed on Thursday morning! The tube has definitely prevented me from more than the trach did, but it's a big relief to be breathing normally again. Its been pretty difficult not speaking or eating whole foods but I only have two days left!

RILEY ALLISON, Carley's sister

Lots of people were reaching out to Car at the hospital, asking how they could help, how they could donate. She eventually started telling people to donate to the oncology unit. I worked at the farmers market, and the woman who ran it, Lesley, used to be our strength trainer for figure skating. Before she got sick, Carley used to busk at the farmers market. So it came up that Lesley offered space to host an event at the farmers market for Carley, just as we were trying to figure out where to direct all the people who wanted to help. Because Carley used to sing at the farmers market, we decided to host a concert fund-raiser. We had a lot of support from the farmers, and we had tents donated, and lots of prizes. Every family friend came, and it was amazing — we didn't raise a ton of money that first year, but the energy and excitement were amazing. It was really the start of our Carley's Angels Foundation.

It was seven days after Carley's last surgery, and seeing those people there to support her gave us all energy to keep going. It was overwhelming.

CARLEY

Today is the Concert for Carley. Don't tell anyone, but right this moment I have tears in my eyes. I'm wearing black shorts and a short gray T-shirt, and my bobbed blond wig. In my bag I have my T-tube supplies. And of course I'm wearing sunglasses, which I have on to cover my eyes — I don't want everyone to see me crying. I'm standing at the back of the field, the sun falling over everything like golden water. Everywhere I look I see someone who loves me. My mom is over there, chatting with Sammy. They lean into each other, gaining strength or perhaps relaxing after the last few months. Riley is busy organizing stuff — she's pulled all this together, and right now she's standing next to the guys from the band, which is about to perform. There's clearly some minor tech issue that they have to figure out.

She must feel me staring at her, because she turns and beckons me over.

I walk toward her, passing my friends from school, passing people I've met at SickKids, passing endless cousins, aunts and uncles … I feel so loved right now. I feel so thankful. I would have never known before this all happened to me, never understood how many people are here for me.

I have a black thought — black thoughts come sometimes. I wonder if these are all the people who would have come to my funeral if I hadn't beaten this. I run my hand up to my throat. The black thought evaporates in the golden light — there at my fingertips is the last trace of everything that's happened. The T-tube will come out in a few days — it's been there since the trach was removed, and soon it will be gone. There will be a small scar and then only the memories.

I see my dad, who is walking over to my mom. He is smiling. It is so good to see him smiling. He isn't thinking about cancer right now; he's just loving having all these people around, and he's loving that this is all over. I am so grateful for my parents — seriously, I had no idea just a few months ago how awesome they are. I just ignored them before all this happened — not in a rude way, but I was busy with my life, busy with my stuff; they were just the background of my grade twelve year. Now I realize they aren't the background but the backbone.

I reach Riley and put my hand on her shoulder.

"Ready?" I ask her.

"Sooo ready."

She gives me a look that is a mix of stressed and excited. She is in her element. I have the sudden vision of her as an actual grown-up. I mean, she is a grown-up already, but suddenly she looks like one. And one day, she'll have kids and be a mom and have some great job and people doing the things she wants them to, because she's always so full of ideas.

I hug her quickly. "This is so amazing, Ri-Ri."

"What's amazing is that you're better."

"Hopefully, today will raise some money for other kids going through stuff like that."

"Exactly." She nods at the band members. They are waiting for the signal. The concert is about to begin.

With an explosion of sound and joy, the music starts.

I've known the whole time where John is standing. It is as if a silvery string links us; when he moves, it tugs at me; when I move, it must tug at him. No one else can see this string, but it is there between us. Just in the moment that the music starts, he walks toward me. I take off my sunglasses. I can tell from the brief expression of concern on his face that he's guessing I have shed a few tears.

"I'm just really happy," I say. "Don't worry."

"I'm really happy, too," he says.

I lean into him, and he leans into me. Support. And relief.

CARLEY'S BLOG

T-Tube gone!
Posted on July 26, 2013

Earlier this morning I had an hour-long surgery to remove the T-Tube. It feels amazing to finally be free from tubes in my trachea, I'm definitely starting to feel more and more like myself again. Luckily I only have to stay in the hospital for one night and I will be back up at the cottage this weekend!

Thank you to everyone for your love and support. I wouldn't be where I am today without all of you. ♥

As for my voice, my parents and I spoke with my doctors today and they explained that my normal voice can take up to a year to get back to the way it was before. I know that I won't be singing for a while and It's hard to imagine my life without it. I was disappointed after hearing this news, but soon realized that if the only thing that is going to affect me for a while will be a raspy voice, I'd say I'm pretty lucky.

CARLEY

I am so happy to be home again — this time with the T-tube OUT. I am like a kid in a candy store — and I'm totally going to eat all the candy. Well, I'm going to eat the Skor Blizzard that John is bringing me, and then I'm going to watch *DodgeBall* with him, and then I'm going to sleep in my own bed, and then I'm going to wake up and start figuring out the rest of my life. I know, I know, I have to start radiation. But not for a while. And for now, I'm going to live every single moment with the most gratitude and intensity I can. I have my birthday party coming up — I think I'm going to wear something gorgeous that makes me look well, and I'm going to forbid anyone from talking about cancer. Not. One. Dirty. Word.

But first, I'm going to hug my family. I'm going to hang out with Riley. She's going to make me watch that video of me dancing in the bed with my trach tube — I was dancing to a Luke Bryan song, and she thinks it's hilarious. We've watched it way-too-many times. And every time I watch it I think of all the ice cream I ate in that hospital, and I want to eat more ice cream!

Riley comes into the kitchen. "How are you doing?"

"You are not allowed to ask that," I reply. I beam at her.

"You're crazy." She pours herself a glass of water. "Do you want one? Or tea?"

"Stop it," I say. I get up from the couch. I go to her and wrap my arms around her. She smells of her perfume; her body is light in my arms; even though I'm über skinny right now, she feels as light-boned as a bird. Her hair is long and soft in my face. I brush it away. "You don't need to worry over me. It's gone. It's over."

She pulls back and looks in my face. "I know. It's a habit, I guess."

"Well, it's a bad habit." I smile. "Time to break it."

I head back over to the couch. She brings her water and sits next to me. I realize she is crying.

"No, Ri, what?"

"I just … It was frigging scary when I came into the waiting room and Mom had her head in her hands and the … the whole thing."

I put my arm around her. "Hey, you, I'm here. I'm okay. It's okay. Deep down, I know you just want to watch that video of me dancing."

She giggles. "How did you know?"

"Go on then. One more time. Then I never want to see that trach again."

"I'm glad you're home."

"And I'm glad you looked after me so well. I suppose I should say thank-you."

"You don't need to."

"I will. But you need to stop crying."

"I have." She wipes her eyes. "I mean, I will."

"Thank you, Ri. I love you."

"I love you, too, Car."

"Can we look at swimsuits instead of the video?" I ask. It's worth a try.

"I guess we could do that. You will need a swimsuit for the trip to Europe."

I lean back into the huge, soft couch. "I can't believe I forgot all about it. I mean, it's not that I forgot, but I've just been so busy in the moment, you know, getting through it. I am so excited. And yes, I most definitely need a new swimsuit. At least one. I think I deserve about ten." I grin at her.

She grins back. "I'll buy you a swimsuit."

I giggle. "You won't. Because I'm not sick anymore, so I don't need special treatment. Well, maybe I take that back. I don't need special treatment after you've bought me ten swimsuits."

She jabs me in my ribs. "That actually hurts."

"Suck it up, Car. Welcome back to reality."

We're laughing a lot when John messages to say he's arrived. One Skor Blizzard ready for me. One lifetime ready for me. I could not be happier.

RILEY ALLISON, Carley's sister

For her eighteenth birthday she wore — 'cause, like, she was so skinny at the time — this, like, see-through long skirt, and it was so see-through that she just wore a little, like, not shorts underneath it but, like, a transparent bottom and a little crop top. She looked amazing.

Family! I am the luckiest girl in the world to have sisters like you two xxxx ♥ ♥ ♥ ♥

Then not long after that, we went on a cruise in the Mediterranean. It was a two-week trip, and we went to lots of places. It was before radiation so Carley wasn't fully in remission yet, but she felt pretty good, and she described herself as cancer free. We did a photoshoot on the cruise, and Carley took off her wig — the photos are beautiful.

Life is 10% what happens to you and 90% how you respond. You're only bald once, right? ♥ #honest #embraceit

I just remember the whole trip being about us together as a family. And I remember Carley. We couldn't go to the bar, so we spent a lot of time playing two-person euchre in our room. One night we made another video of us singing and dancing — we were just fooling around. The video is a little graphic. I keep my clothes on, Carley doesn't. This is what we did in the room. She was just so much fun. But the video is embarrassing. We're dancing to Meat Loaf. So, so horrible. So embarrassing.

JOHN SERVINIS, Carley's boyfriend

AUGUST: REGATTA WEEKEND

My most favorite way to spend time! #onthegull

We drove up in the truck; it was the first weekend spending it at the cottage with her family. Carley didn't tell me anything we were going to do or how important this weekend was; the only information I had been given was five minutes before the ride up by her cousins, explaining the canoe races and every competition.

Although I loved to give her surprises, Carley *loved* to put me in uncomfortable situations just to see me panic. She thought it was funny!

I met many of the cousins for the first time and got to experience and see all the things I had missed out on before I was in Carley's life. It gave me an insight into her childhood. I fell in love with her that weekend. I couldn't tell her, though.

SEPTEMBER

I had gone away for university. She visited me for the first time, meeting everyone on my floor, who loved her. I took her for dinner to Jack Astor's that night. We always ordered calamari as an appetizer — it was as if we didn't even need to ask each other. I told her I loved her. She said, "I love you, too." I've never said that to anyone other than her. She hated how often I said it to her after that through our relationship, but I just wanted her to always know how much I loved her.

CARLEY'S BLOG

Updates!
Posted on August 24, 2013

Hey everyone!

Sorry, I haven't written in a while. I've been enjoying all the time I have feeling healthy before I start radiation.

On July 16th, a fundraiser was held in my name to support SickKids (Concert for Carley). I want to thank my sister Riley for organizing the event, and I want to thank everyone who came out to support the SickKids hospital oncology unit. We raised close to $3000!

Next week, I will be going back to the hospital for a meeting with my radiation oncologist. I will be starting radiation at the beginning of September, and I'll continue treatment for six weeks. At this moment we are not sure of what dosage radiation I will be getting but we will have a better idea come next week.

As for how I'm feeling, I feel great! The chemo is slowly running out of my system and I am starting to feel much more like myself. My neck has been healing extremely well and my voice is getting a bit better every day. I know radiation is going to be hard on my throat but it's only for six weeks and then it is all over.

Starting Radiation!
Posted on September 8, 2013

Tomorrow at 9:00 a.m. will be my first radiation treatment. I am nervous for treatment, yet extremely excited that I can finally see the finish line. Like I said before, the four steps of my treatment are just a 400-m track-and-field race, and I've only got 100 m left!

♥

Radiation Day 2
Posted on September 10, 2013

I just finished my second day of radiation and I am still feeling good! The radiation therapy is much different than I thought it would be, although I didn't really know what to expect to begin with. The treatment itself is kinda like having an MRI or CT scan, except the radiation is specifically targeted in one spot. To help me keep in place I have to wear a mask that is tied down to the table. The mask starts at the top of my chest and reaches to the top of my head. I'd say that is probably the most uncomfortable part of it all, and for about twenty minutes after radiation I have the imprint of the mask on my face. But I guess I can deal with that.

Two down thirty-one more to go!

On another note, the chemo is almost all out of my system and my hair has started to grow back!

♥

Radiation Week 2
Posted on September 18, 2013

Halfway through week two of radiation and I'm still feeling pretty good, although I have a killer sore throat. I've been able to keep up with my day-to-day schedule ever since I started radiation, but it is beginning to get difficult as the radiation goes on. I've been back on the ice for the last two weeks and I'm hoping to stay on the ice through the radiation treatment.

One and a half weeks down, five to go!

I finally rode my horse for the first time today since I've been sick!

so happy to be reunited with my baby girl

♥

Radiation Week 4
Posted on October 1, 2013

Sixteen out of thirty-three done!

Just under halfway and I'm feeling alright. Some things

have changed though, my throat hasn't gotten worse but I have completely lost my sense of taste. Last night after dinner I decided I wanted to have chocolate ... just to find it tasted like cardboard. So eating isn't really an enjoyable thing these days but at least I am still physically able to.

I'm still on the ice every day training for Sectionals in November and things are going really well. And I am extremely excited about my new short program to Swan Lake.

I may not feel great, but I only have seventeen more to go! I can see the finish line!

RILEY ALLISON, Carley's sister

It was just so good to see her getting better and to see her getting closer to being done. We could feel it moving into the past, and it was awesome to start getting on with our lives again. I loved it when I could go with her on the ice — it felt like it used to, but different, too. We loved it more than before, I guess.

CARLEY'S BLOG

8 months gone by
Posted on October 2, 2013

- 8 months since diagnosis
- 8 months since Tracheotomy Surgery
- 7 months since I started Chemotherapy
- 5 months since I finished Chemotherapy
- 3 months since the Operation
- 2 months since T-Tube removal
- and finally 3 and a half weeks into Radiation

It's hard to believe that it's been eight months since the diagnosis. Time has certainly flown by. I was in the hospital for two weeks straight after the diagnosis, and thinking back on those two weeks I realize that they were two incredible weeks. Those two weeks showed me how extremely special my family is, those two weeks showed me what amazing friends I have, and those two weeks changed my perspective on everything. The things that seemed to matter the most before February 4th aren't even close to my biggest concerns anymore.

The four months I spent at Sick Children's Hospital was an eye-opener. Without firsthand experience at the oncology ward at SickKids you will never be able to understand how incredibly strong and beautiful these kids are. Although at the time it may have seemed like the days could not get any longer and the pain was never-ending, I now know I only have two and a half weeks left and this will all be in my past.

And the feeling of being back on the ice is indescribable. Feels just like it should at this time of year getting ready for the Central Ontario Championships.

♥

Radiation Week 5
Posted on October 9, 2013

Almost done week 5!

After my treatment today, I only have ten radiation days left! Almost into the single digits.

I was told that by this time in my treatment, I would be in bed almost all the time, feeling very sick, unable to swallow any food, and that I'd probably lose weight again. I am proud to say that I have not lost a pound since I started radiation! I am still able to skate every day, and I have actually gotten used to my sore throat. And my diet is relatively normal.

But I can't wait until October 23, my last day of radiation and the end of the final stage in beating this thing!

♥

Radiation Week 6!
Posted on October 16, 2013

Halfway through my last full week of radiation! This week was a little different because I had two treatments instead of one on Tuesday. Having one treatment is tiring enough but having two really pushed me over the edge yesterday. Although they were six hours apart it was still very demanding on my body.

I'm feeling a lot of the effects from the radiation these days but I only have five treatments left! My voice has gotten a bit worse but it's not exactly backtracking the progression I have made. It sounds more like a laryngitis than anything.

I've still been skating every day and I'm looking forward to competing soon! Things are finally starting to come together, and I'm excited to get back out there and compete.

One week from today will be my last radiation treatment, and the last of all my treatments! I can't wait to feel like myself again! It's crazy to think it's almost all over.

♥

And the 3-day Countdown Begins ...
Posted on October 20, 2013

I can't wait to tackle this week and be done with radiation forever! Home stretch!

♥

2 days to go!
Posted on October 21, 2013

I'm almost there! I've almost completed all thirty-three radiation treatments. Today I'm feeling pretty sick but I know I only have two left! Today we met with my Radiation Oncologist and I finally realized this was going to be the last time I meet with him in that office after a radiation treatment. It was kind of a weird thing to wrap my head around. I've gotten so used to going down to Princess Margaret every day, sitting in the same chair, waiting for radiation, having radiation, then going to see my doctor once a week.

It's all become part of my daily routine.

But I am so excited and so thankful that Wednesday is going to be my last day!

Be stronger than your excuses.

♥

Eleven Hours till I ...
Posted on October 23, 2013

Eleven hours till I'm done with treatment forever!

CHAPTER SEVEN

Spend time with the good memories;
hold them close in your heart.

— Carley

CARLEY'S BLOG

150% Cancer Free
Posted on October 23, 2013

Ten months ago I was diagnosed with a clear cell sarcoma in the trachea. Knowing it was the second case in the world, we knew it was going to be a tough fight.

1. Emergency Tracheotomy surgery
2. PICC line operation
3. 6 rounds of Chemotherapy (3 months)
4. Tracheal surgery (7 hours)
5. T-Tube removal surgery
6. PICC line removal
7. 6 weeks of radiation

Here I am ten months later and I'm still trying to live my

normal life. I've been training every day since September and I'm competing in two weeks. I don't have my long blond hair but I have a substitute. I have countless scars on my body from surgeries and needles but they are only skin deep.

I can finally say I KICKED CANCER'S ASS! It's been quite the journey and such an incredible experience. Thank you to everyone who has been there for me and supported me through everything. I can't thank you all enough. I would not be the person I am today without all of you. Thank you to all of my doctors for getting me healthy and never doubting what I was capable of.

From here on, it's a new beginning and I can't wait to get started. "Scars are tattoos with better stories." I don't know who said this first, but it's one of my favorite quotations. My scar is a part of me now and it will always remind me of what I am capable of.

SAMANTHA ALLISON, Carley's sister

Celebrating my beautiful sis Sammy on her birthday.
Couldn't have got through this without you.
#cancerfree

When Carley finished radiation on October 23, 2013, our family went out to dinner for my birthday. We went to JOEY — Carley's favorite restaurant. We were all sitting, finishing our food, when Dad stood up. He gave a short speech, saying how these last eight months had taught us all so much as a family.

Then he opened up a box, and he gave me, my mom, Carley and Riley a bracelet each. On each bracelet was a charm that read *I Love You*. He got himself a charm, too, to wear around his neck. He said the gift was to remind us of the past year and how close we had all become.

It was a perfect moment.

CARLEY

As the day ends, I spend about an hour creating a picture time-line of everything that happened during my cancer journey. I share it on my blog. I message Denzelle and John — I miss them all so much now that they are all at university and I'm here at home still, not with them, where I was supposed to be. I especially miss John. He's so good-looking that I know all the girls there will just be throwing themselves at him. He reassures me all the time that he adores me, but sometimes I wonder if he'd be happier with someone who hadn't had to deal with this cancer journey. I put the negative ideas out of my head. I focus on the fact that I'll be there next year. I can't wait until I'm at university and not stuck here, although Mom has talked to me about working at the car dealership for now, and I'm excited to start doing that.

It's dark and cold outside — if I press my hand to the window, the glass is freezing. I picture myself bundled up in the snow; perhaps we can go snowboarding this year. I love the feel of racing down a mountain slope, my stomach tight, my body leaning, the board swooshing up sprays of snow and plunging over icy patches.

I have the house to myself, which is unusual. Normally, there are so many people here and I hardly have to sit with my thoughts — but I'm noticing that now that the cancer has gone, my thoughts are okay. I've been thinking about sharing with the people who read my blog a few ideas about things I've learned during my cancer journey. Everything is so different for me now — I know so much more than I did before I was sick. I guess I've been thinking about this since the interview with Dad. It was super fun — we sat together and he filmed me, and we talked about my diagnosis and my life. I felt a bit like a celebrity, but one who has a really important message to share. Both Dad and I think it's important to record everything we've been through as a family. Sometimes, I look at my parents, and I see how their faces have changed — they are a gorgeous couple, but there's something compelling about their faces now. Almost like they know that life isn't all sunshine and roses. They have been through pain, more pain than I have, that's for sure.

I move from the kitchen to the music room. I move quietly, almost like a ghost. A happy ghost, spending time in the places I most love. I can't really believe this part of my journey is over — I almost don't know what to do with myself. I'm so used to having to deal with cancer, to having to talk about it, to having to live with the day-to-day uncertainty, that now that it's over, I'm not sure who I am anymore.

I drift out of the music room and head upstairs. I pause to look at the wall of photographs — my family has some fantastic pictures of us all on this wall. I look at a picture of my parents when they were younger, and then at one of my sisters and me as kids. I head into my room and take out my sports gear for the morning. Tomorrow, Dad and I will make sure the video is transferred to a computer, and I will be back on the ice. I've decided to compete for sectionals — I'm going to be the best I can be.

♥

Downstairs, I hear my mom open the side door. She calls my name. Her voice floats up the stairs.

"I'm here, Mom."

Her face breaks into a smile when she sees me come around the corner of the kitchen. For a moment, I see her as she would have been when she was much younger. I am so happy to see her happy.

I hug her tight. She holds me close.

This would be a secret for living: enjoy those you love.

MARK ALLISON, Carley's dad, interviews **CARLEY**

MARK: When were you diagnosed and with what type of cancer?

CARLEY: I was diagnosed on February 4, 2013, which was also my dad's fiftieth birthday, and at the time the diagnosis was a malignant melanoma. But over time the pathology was reviewed by the doctors; it turned out to be clear cell sarcoma.

MARK: How did you handle and react to your diagnosis?

CARLEY: So, I actually wasn't told off the bat what was going on, and I was ... I feel like I was eased into it. I started hearing talk about a lump and talk about a disease ... a rare disease, and I only really found through pieces through everyone what was actually going on. So for me, one day, I woke up and was like, "Oh, wow this is my reality now."

MARK: How does your illness affect your family?

CARLEY: So my illness greatly affected my family. We had to change lots of things around the house. My parents' work schedules had to change to accommodate me. My sister had to take some time off school. It was hard to function normally as a family, but you know, we did our best, and I'm just so grateful for all the things they did for me throughout that whole period of time.

MARK: How did your illness affect your everyday life?

CARLEY: When I got sick and I had to be pulled out of school, I wasn't skating and I couldn't sing. It was very different for me. I had to learn a slow-paced lifestyle, which I had never experienced before, but I got used to it, and now I'm starting to put things back to normal, so I'm learning how to live two different lifestyles.

MARK: Do you feel that your illness has changed you as a person?

CARLEY: I appreciate every little thing now. I mean simple things like going to a restaurant and being able to eat anything I want. But for the six months or eight months I was going through treatment, I couldn't do that. I couldn't just pick anything — I had to think, Is it pureed enough? Is it too spicy? Just to have the freedom to do normal things feels like a huge opportunity for me. It feels amazing to just do things normally the way a normal person would.

MARK: Do you do anything different today that you didn't do before you were diagnosed?

CARLEY: I noticed when I had a tracheostomy — the hole in my neck with a tube so I could breathe — I noticed when I went out in public, sometimes people ... it was almost like a disability or handicap. When people look at people, at their disabilities or their handicap, they stare. I experienced that firsthand, and although mine was only for a period of a few months, I did get to experience it, and I think I have a better understanding of how to react to people with handicaps than I did before. I understand it better, and you just treat them like everybody else. You don't give it a second glance. And that's one thing I definitely do every day in my life that I wouldn't have before I was diagnosed.

MARK: If you could send a message to other people suffering from cancer, what would you say?

CARLEY: You just have to remember that everyone is there for you all the time. Your family, your friends, everyone is on your side, and you will get through it. And it's just one of those things. Never, never put the doubts in your mind. Never think, Oh, well, I'm really, really not feeling well. Always think, Tomorrow I'll be better than I was today. Think forward, think ahead — you'll get better in the end. You gotta keep that in mind.

SHIN AMANO, Carley's skating coach

Her smile — I'll never forget seeing her smile as she got back on the ice.

She was different from before. She thought she was able to do everything right away. When she decided to compete, for her it was no excuses. Training has to be safe, and I had always pushed her, but now … now I didn't even need to push her. She already did that. Before I even said something, she knew what I was speaking about. She was much easier to train, better.

thanks for being the best coach #amazingcoach

Then Carley had sectionals. To me, the moment she stepped on the ice I thought she was a champion. But Carley wasn't feeling good about her performance. She was all about appraisement — she wanted to do better, but I was just happy to see she was on the ice, and I was so proud of her. I was very emotional.

Then we were trying to go over the next section for the next season, and she trained until she was able to do two and a half revolutions in the air, and we decided to train with that for the next competition. She was just pushing more than usual.

BRYAN AULD, Carley's high school principal

I remember seeing her when she went back to skate competitively. She clearly wasn't in 100 percent shape. She clearly wasn't going to do as well. She was frustrated with herself, but even at that stage, she was so determined and so passionate, and it wasn't about "Hey, I've had cancer. I should just really be happy for the fact that I'm here competing." It was "No, why did I just fall? Why am I not able to do that? I don't care that I've got cancer. I'm not cutting myself any breaks here. I should be my best, and I'm not," and she was pissed off with herself.

That determination was so real with her. Be your best. Always. And always smile, which to me doesn't mean just being happy. It means determination. It means being satisfied not just with your best but satisfied with what you have and appreciating what you have. Appreciating the love of family, love of friends, and just being a good person.

CARLEY'S BLOG

Sectionals!
Posted on November 10, 2013

Sectionals began on Friday night when I did my short program. As much as I said I didn't expect anything out of myself, I definitely did. We finished the choreography for the short program much earlier than we finished the long program, so I felt I was most prepared for the short. After I competed I was very disappointed with myself. I didn't land all my jumps and my spins were not their best. I started to wonder if I had really pushed myself to compete for nothing. I wondered if every day I stayed in bed all day and just made myself wake up and get up so I could skate was worth it. But after being upset for a while, I quickly realized I needed to put things into perspective. I have been off the ice for eight months and I wasn't exactly taking a vacation. So I tried to forget about Friday as I moved into Saturday. Saturday was my long program and I knew I was really going to have to focus. The program was only finished two weeks ago and it was already time to compete. But most importantly I wanted to have fun, I wanted to get back on the competition ice after a long year and remind myself that I kicked cancer's butt. I began my long program with a smile on my face and I enjoyed every minute of it, and it turned out to be a very good skate. I didn't have the same level of difficulty in my jumps as most of my competitors, but that's not what this competition was about for me anyways. I just wanted to get myself back out there and enjoy myself because I think I deserve to smile after such a tough battle.

♥

6 Week checkup!
Posted on December 4, 2013

Yesterday I had a six-week-post-radiation follow up with my radiation oncologist, and today I had an appointment with my surgeon. Things are starting to get much better, but I have developed a brutal cough. My radiation oncologist explained that the radiation affected the top portions of my lungs and they have been a bit irritated. Generally patients will develop this cough a few months after radiation but since mine has come much earlier we suspect I am healing much faster.

I am extremely happy I am starting to get better but some days it feels like this is all dragging on forever. I just want to wake up one day and feel perfectly healthy but I know it's going to take some time.

Other than doctors' appointments and voice therapy, I've been busy getting on with my life, hanging out with John, healing and skating! I'm getting ready for the Olympic Dreams ice show!

JOHN SERVINIS, Carley's boyfriend

In the fall of 2013, I was visiting. Carley and I went to see a family friend of hers who is a very close friend of the owner of the Bowmanville Zoo. We went over, played with the baby lions. We loved to go on spontaneous dates — I organized a date to Ripley's Aquarium and other stuff like that. I liked to surprise her.

I remember one night she had no idea where we were going. I had booked the 360 Restaurant on top of the CN Tower a month in advance, at a time when the sun would set midway through our meal. It didn't go to plan, as it had rained that day. We talked about our future together that night and how far we had come. To me, she didn't seem that different after what she'd been through. She was always the type of person who was goal driven; once one task was accomplished, she would move on to the next until she was able to reach what she wanted to achieve.

But during the fall we had a couple of fights, because I couldn't visit due to school. She was jealous in terms of the girls on my floor, but we figured it out. Carley and I would fight for ten minutes and then forgive each other. When I realized that, it showed me we were perfect for each other and I was going to be with her for a long time.

DENZELLE HUNTER, Carley's friend

Carley was just always there. She was someone who was very compassionate and willing to listen, and people just loved to talk to her. And we were all so happy that everything was back to normal. We all were coming home for Christmas, and I couldn't wait to spend time with Carley.

CARLEY

I love Christmas. Not quite as much as my dad, who we call "Mr. Christmas" and who decorates our front yard with lights and this year a blow-up Santa. But I love it. I love the way our house smells like cooking. I love dressing up and doing my makeup. I love that all my friends are coming home and there will be parties and time to hang out. I love exchanging presents with the Reddick girls, and I love buying the absolutely perfect present for everyone. I've been planning John's present for ages. It feels like a small way to say thank-you for everything that everyone was for me through this whole journey.

Riley and I spend an hour in her room laughing our heads off at a video of the two of us dancing. We're both crazy, flinging our heads around and laughing. Sammy comes in and shares a picture of the three of us in a crib when we were babies — well, she was a baby; we were both a bit bigger. She says, "I don't think we'd all fit in there this year."

We're all giggly and silly, and then we decide to get dressed up, even though we're not going anywhere tonight. We decide it's a practice run for all the Christmas parties. I put on a long black dress. Riley chooses a black dress, too, and Sammy picks a blue one. We fool around with hair and makeup, moving into my room, where I have a great couple of mirrors in my bathroom. I say, "I guess from January 2013 to now it just looks like I got a haircut," and Sammy gives me an extra-big hug.

We listen to music and chat — I even tell them that I'm nervous about my Olympic Dreams show coming up on the ice, and they both reassure me that I'll be great.

Riley catches my eye in the mirror. I know what she's thinking.

Everything. Is. Just. So. Normal. It's perfect.

JOHN SERVINIS, Carley's boyfriend

She was the first girl I had ever brought home to my family. She came for the Christmas parties my family would throw, and I went to hers. I went to Uncle Dave's house and met a lot of the family. She came over to my house for Christmas Day. Her grandparents had passed away already, so she enjoyed trying to talk to my grandparents. She listened to my grandpa ramble for thirty minutes while the rest of the family watched and laughed. She came back telling me she had no idea what he was talking about. She was trying so hard to be liked by my family and endured my grandpa's rambling. My grandparents told me she was very beautiful and they liked her a lot. I knew she was the one that night.

CHAPTER EIGHT

It's about the decisions you
make every single day.
— Carley

CARLEY'S BLOG

CT Results!
Posted on January 22, 2014

Today I met with my oncologist to discuss the results of my CT scan. Before the doctor came in today, a young lady came in and informed us that my doctor would be coming in shortly and we will be talking about participating in a Clinical Trial. My parents didn't really say anything and the woman left the room. Their minds immediately went to the worst-case scenario, thinking my cancer had returned and they wanted to try a new treatment. A few moments later the lady came back into our room and said, "Oh my gosh, I'm so sorry. I meant to give that news to another patient."

I could hear both my parents give a sigh of relief as my mom put her head in her hands and shed a few tears of joy. My doctor came into the room and said everything on the scan looked great and I am still clear of cancer! We discussed a number of things today which included the statistical value for recurrence. They mentioned that if the scans remain clear for a period of two years after diagnosis (Feb. 2015) then the chances of recurrence are exponentially lowered. I will be scanned for the next year every three months, then after the year, every six months. I'm crossing my fingers to keep the good results coming!

Thank you for all the love and support!

♥

More good news!
Posted on January 23, 2014

Today my parents and I met with my surgeon. We went over the results of the CT Scan and he sent a scope down my airway. He was so excited to see how well things were healing and how smooth the incision looked from the inside. It's always comforting when my surgeon is excited to give us results. He looked at me and said, "Everything looks perfect!"

He watched a few videos of me skating and was astonished by how much movement I had back in my neck already. Things are definitely looking bright!

♥

Almost 1 Year!
Posted on February 3, 2014

Tomorrow is the one-year mark since I was diagnosed! I cannot believe that it has been a full year, but I can definitely say it has been the most eventful year of my life. On this day last year, I was at home because the hospital told me I had a small hole in my lung and that it would heal in a few days so I should just rest at home. I remember this day last year very clearly because I could not fall asleep. I was home on the couch all day but I wasn't able to sleep because I couldn't catch my breath. I had also gotten very skinny by this point last year and family and friends were concerned for my health. I am very excited to reach the one-year mark since I was diagnosed and celebrate not only for successfully making it to one year, but also to give my dad a REAL 50th Birthday. As many of you know I was diagnosed on my Dad's 50th Birthday. I think I gave him the worst 50th Birthday gift a dad could ask for last year, but I know this year is going to be all smiles for all of us.

I know my dad is going to have a wonderful second 50th Birthday. :)

♥

ONE YEAR!
Posted on February 4, 2014

Before I got sick I had seen this quote that said, "When someone has cancer, their family and everyone who loves them gets cancer too." I never understood it.

Ever since I got sick and I got to experience firsthand how

someone's cancer can affect the entire family I started to understand. My cancer affected everyone around me, my family had to put their lives on hold to help me through this and I cannot express how much I appreciate them.

Thank you to my sisters for the amazing messages today!

Well, Baby girl. It has been one year since I received that phone call, one year since we traded our beds for hospital floors, one year since you traded the diva clothes for a hospital gown and one year from when you showed the world just what a little Allison girl is made of. You can even see from the photos, here is a concerned, scared big sis and there is a lil sis just making the best of every moment! Words cannot describe how strong you were last year getting everyone and yourself through! You kicked cancer's ass, and that is that!!!

Love, your biggest sister and biggest fan ♥

I ♥ *you*

— Riley!

ps Happy 50th Dad (round 2)

♥

World Cancer Day!
Posted on February 5, 2014

Last night I was on my phone doing a few things and I saw a picture on Instagram from PMH (Princess Margaret Hospital). It mentioned that yesterday was World Cancer Day! What are the odds of being diagnosed on World Cancer Day! Now that's one more thing to add to the list of coincidental things landing on significant dates through my cancer journey!

> February 4th
> - World Cancer Day
> - Dad's Birthday
> - Diagnosed

> October 23rd
> - Sammy's Birthday
> - The day I finished treatment

♥

Back at TGH
Posted on February 6, 2014

Today my dad and I went down to Toronto General Hospital for an appointment with the endocrinologist. I've only really been to TGH for two other occasions, first being my tumor-removal surgery, second being my T-tube removal surgery. So, it was a bit strange going there just for an appointment. As I walked through the front doors I walked by the ice cream shop I used to go to while I was recovering from surgery. I can still remember spending hours trying to finish my ice cream because everything was so hard for me to swallow. It makes me appreciate the simple things, and how far I have come since July!

As for the meeting with the endocrinologist, everything is great! We adjusted the dosage of my thyroid medication, and spoke about how I have been feeling in general. I'm so glad everything is well and I'm back to living my normal life. Well sort of. It's back to my normal life plus A LOT more appointments.

♥

Such a great email
Posted on April 3, 2014

Such an uplifting email I got from one of our close family friends Michael Nadel! Thank you Amanda for being awesome! It's an amazing feeling to know that I've made an impact on people's lives, even if it's just family and friends.

P.S. Coincidence or not my 6-year-old daughter Amanda came into my room this morning... she was wearing the Concert for Carley shirt as a nightie. Apparently, Amanda was doing a survey at school yesterday asking her classmates who they like the most: Justin Bieber, Katy Perry or Carley Allison. Albeit most of the respondents to her survey were familiar with Justin Bieber & Katy Perry, four people (including Amanda) knew Carley and picked her as their favorite star...

I don't know where she picked up on all this vibe but she is so excited to wear her Carley shirt to school.
— Michael Nadel

LYNDSAY REDDICK, Carley's friend

Carley's mom's family owns car dealerships. So, Carley began working for her family; she was working in the office. She worked reception, but she had a little bit more responsibility than that, and she really liked it. She wanted to go to Queen's for business so that she could start working with her family because she really loved it. She was really good at it, and I think that was one of the best years of her life. Even though her friends were away, she went to visit her boyfriend, John, all the time. She said to me once, "I've been through chemo now, so John and I will have to have kids young because I might not be as fertile when I'm older." She was always having plans for the future.

JOHN SERVINIS, Carley's boyfriend

On Valentine's Day I skipped my Friday classes so that I could jump on a train at 5:30 a.m. to see Carley and be in Toronto by 8:30 a.m. I went straight to her house and gave her roses. We then took our sisters and their friends downtown, where our plans changed. Coincidentally we ended up having lunch in the same restaurant as them. Due to the lack of sleep from studying for midterms and from the train ride and travel, I felt sick, and we left. I ended up falling asleep while we were in traffic for three hours on the way back to her house. She woke me up when we had stopped in her garage, gave me a kiss, said I was cute and then made me feel bad in front of her family for falling asleep. It made me love her even more. I ended up spending the rest of the day at the Allisons'. I was planning on ordering wings with Carley and just watching a movie like we would always do, but Mark insisted on going to dinner all together. I think this was better. We went to a Persian restaurant, and even though it wasn't a date, I got to spend it with her family, laughing.

She apologized for us having to spend our Valentine's Day with her family. I said I loved her family and never to apologize for them.

"Darling,"
an original song by Carley Allison
Published on April 7, 2014

"When I'm alone, sometimes I dream of how it used to be.
Before I was tested on how strong, how strong I'd be.
For one day, I woke up to a new reality. I start to think, Is
it worth it, putting up with pain?
The never-ending unknown what the next day was going
to bring for me.
There came a day I found out just how serious things
could be.

My mama looked at me, wiped her tears and said, 'Don't
shed a tear, my darling.
I know that you'll be strong. And don't ever think twice, my
darling, you can cry here in my arms.'
So, both and Mom and Dad go through this. 'Why do I
have to see my baby girl?
And we know you're no ordinary — you're a fighter, and
you'll fight strong.'

When you got that call, you looked at me, tears running
down your face.
The doctor told you that they wanted to try something not
so ordinary.
I sat there in shock with you. And wondered what this
would mean for me.
But three months passed by, but I just wanted my old life back.

*My mama looked at me, wiped her tears and said, 'Don't
    shed a tear, my darling.*
*I know that you'll be strong. And don't ever think twice, my
    darling, you can cry here in my arms.'*
*So both Mom and Dad go through this. 'Why do I have to
    see my baby girl?*
*And we know you're no ordinary — you're a fighter, and
    you'll fight strong.'*

*Don't know what to say. Don't know what to do. Some
    times I break. Sometimes I break.*

I won't shed a tear. Don't worry. And I'll try to be strong.
*And I won't think twice, don't worry, but I might cry in
    your arms."*

CARLEY'S BLOG

6 Month Checkup!
Posted on May 5, 2014

Tomorrow I will be going to Princess Margaret to meet with my oncologist to discuss the results of my CT scan. I had my scan about two weeks ago and I have been very anxious to see the results!

As for how I'm doing ... I have been feeling great! I have noticed that my energy levels are getting better and better every month. I can finally last a full day and late night without feeling like I was going to need to sleep for the next few days. My thyroid medication is still giving me troubles but we are in the middle of having it all figured out. I am meeting with the endocrinologist Wednesday afternoon to discuss what the problem may be.

I will keep you all updated when I get the results of the scan!

xoxo

♥

CT Scan Results!
Posted on May 7, 2014

Yesterday I got the results from my CT scan and ... Cancer free!!! SOooo happy and excited to know that the scans show no evidence of recurrence. They also show significant healing in my tracheal area! It's always nice to see my oncologist and get these good results. We still meet my oncologist in the same room as we did during my chemotherapy. And I still remember the days we would go in for an appointment extremely anxious to see if the chemo was affecting my tumor. Even though it was a year ago, it still feels like just yesterday.

I'm currently seeing my voice therapist and we are working on getting my singing voice back!

We met with an endocrinologist today to check my thyroid levels and I was a bit lower than the average, so I understand why I haven't been feeling great recently. We got it sorted out and I should be feeling better soon!

MICHAEL NADEL, family friend

On June 4, 2014, Carley appeared on the Global TV breakfast show with her surgeon, Dr. Patrick Gullane, a recipient of the Order of Canada, who had performed the surgery on her trachea (https://globalnews.ca/video/1373172/carley-allison/).

On June 7, 2014, Carley sang the national anthem to kick off the 2014 Princess Margaret Hospital Foundation's Ride to Conquer Cancer. A team consisting of her mother, father and other friends and family participated in the two-day, 200-plus-kilometer ride from Exhibition Place in Toronto to Niagara Falls, Ontario, to help raise over $20 million for cancer research.

Hey everyone! A team of friends & family are doing the PMH Ride to Conquer Cancer! Please support us!

JOHN SERVINIS, Carley's boyfriend

When Carley sang at the Ride to Conquer Cancer, she wore this yellow dress. It was a really nice yellow dress. It was, like, conservative, like something you would imagine someone wearing to a polo match. Forever I can see this moment in my head — her, just looking at me and then giving me a kiss. I just remember every single detail of that.

CARLEY'S BLOG

Ride to Conquer Cancer!
Posted on June 7, 2014

This morning I sang the national anthem in the opening ceremonies for the Ride to Conquer Cancer. I had such an amazing time and I met so many inspirational people. Last night me, my dad, and sister Riley went down to Ontario Place grounds for the rehearsal. I stood at the edge of the stage waiting for my cue, while Paul Alofs introduced me. Hearing Paul tell my story brought back a lot of memories. I thought to myself, One year ago today, I was lying in bed recovering from my last round of chemo, and today I'm standing here ready to sing.

When I had my surgery last summer, I didn't know if I would ever sing again. At the time, my voice wasn't my biggest concern: I needed to have the surgery to save my life. After the surgery I could not talk properly for a few months, and when I started talking a bit again, the radiation took my voice right back to where it was after surgery.

To stand on the stage today and sing the national anthem for cancer survivors and supporters was such an amazing feeling. I have such mixed feelings when I think back on my cancer experience, but today it was clear to me that I have reached the goal I set out to achieve with my story and blog. I started writing my blog for a few reasons, one being to give other cancer fighters hope and inspiration to keep fighting. Hearing the words "You're my inspiration" is one of the greatest feelings in the entire world.

Cancer took away one year of my life, but it has given me so much more. I feel so fortunate to have had such amazing care at SickKids, PMH and TGH.

Thank you again everyone for all of your support. I have the most amazing friends and family in the entire world.

♥

Ride to Conquer Cancer National Anthem!
June 9, 2014

Such an honor to be a part of this incredible weekend! Although my voice isn't the way it used to be and I'm still trying to get used to it I was happy I could sing the anthem to kick off the event!

VIDEO: Ride to Conquer Cancer — National Anthem by Carley Allison
www.youtube.com/watch?v=1k7f3JigwSc

You have to fight through some bad days, to earn the best days of your life #familyfightstogether #curingcarley #thatsme

Concert for Carley 2014!

Posted on June 24, 2014

Hey everyone!

This year we will be having our second annual Concert for Carley! It will be held at the apple [Appletree] markets June Rowlings [Rowlands] park location on July 15! The concert will be held from 4-7! Come out to enjoy some live music and fresh foods from the market!

Also! Coming up in just over a week will be the anniversary of my surgery! Hard to believe at this time last year the thought of being "cancer free" was just around the corner!

Xoxo
Carley

RILEY ALLISON, Carley's sister

The major difference between the first Concert for Carley and this second one was that Carley performed at the second one.

She performed a song with Sarah, and then she performed two or three songs by herself. One of the songs was "Skinny Love." She was totally fine at this point, but her voice had dropped, and she was still learning how to sing with this new voice. For her, it was a small stage, but it was an opportunity to test out her new instrument, her voice. Everyone was there to support her, and it was the best environment for her. Because of the hype from the first concert, the vendors at the farmers market were excited to see her perform. It was awesome.

CARLEY'S BLOG

PMH Event!
Posted on June 26, 2014

I wanted to give a big thank you to everyone who came to the event at PMH last Wednesday. It was such a great feeling to have all of you gathered to celebrate and honor my wonderful doctors and support team.

The event last Wednesday was the first time in a long time that I have heard my story told out loud. I find that as I've gradually gotten healthier, I've gradually gotten more sensitive to the thoughts of my past year. I think part of it is because every time someone used to ask me "How are you doing?" or "How are you feeling?" my answer would always be "I'm great!" or "I'm doing well!" and when I think back on those times I realize I was far from great and definitely wasn't doing well. But at the time, that's what great felt like.

I was thinking back on last year at this time and I was trying to remember what it felt like, but I was having a hard time remembering. They say your mind suppresses traumatic experiences, and I think the week before surgery was definitely a feeling my brain didn't want me to remember. The feeling of the unknown was the scariest for my family and me.

Not knowing if they could remove the tumor, not knowing if I would live with a trach for the rest of my life.

But I left my life in the hands of my amazing doctors and we couldn't have asked for better results. It's crazy to think it's almost been a full year since the big operation, but it's safe to say my family and I are all in a much better place this year! Thank you again to everyone who came last Wednesday! It was a wonderful event and I was so glad to share it with everyone.

xo
Carley Elle

♥

One Year since "Success in the OR"
Posted on July 3, 2014

It's hard to believe that it has been one year since I had my surgery. As I sat down at dinner with my family today, I realized that last year at this time, food and a cold glass of water were the only things I wanted. So as I ate dinner today I made sure I didn't take it for granted. For a while after surgery, I could not eat solid foods, and I couldn't drink thin liquids. Cancer has taught me to appreciate the little things in life.

Last year at this time I was ninety pounds, bald and pale. I never realized how much difference a year could make. I am in a much better place now and I owe it all to my support team.

♥

Concert for Carley
Posted on July 14, 2014

Tomorrow is the big day!
Concert starts at 4:00 p.m. and runs until 7:00!
We can't wait to see everyone tomorrow! Thanks in advance to those of you coming tomorrow!

Last year this event was a great hit and I don't expect anything less this year! Hopefully the rain will hold off until after seven! But, if not, we have lots of shelter!

♥

Concert for Carley Success!
Posted on July 18, 2014

Thank you to everyone who came out on Tuesday to Concert for Carley! The rain held off and we had a great day!

My sister Riley is the real brains behind the operation at

Concert for Carley. She has put so much time and effort into making the day go perfectly and she did an amazing job! I cannot thank her enough for making the concert wonderful for a second year in a row and raising close to $2000 for Sick-Kids Hospital Oncology! Riley is truly a remarkable person.

Concert for Carley is going to be an annual event! Riley has so many great ideas and I just know that one day the Concert is going to do great things for the SickKids Oncology unit!

Thank you to all of the amazing volunteers! We couldn't have done it without each and every one of you!

SHIN AMANO, Carley's skating coach

We got a donut spin — so she was skating, and then she is supposed to make a kind of donut ... it looks like donut. She said, "It feels like it cracked or something here." She pointed at her ribs. "So I can't make donut. Can I just not skate the donut? Just not today?"

Carley was always willing to try anything on the ice. So, I was surprised. Worried.

RILEY ALLISON, Carley's sister

Her last competition was Summer Skate 2014, at the beginning of August. All of us were there to watch.

cancer can't shatter passion
#findacureforclearcellsarcoma #fuckcancer

JOHN SERVINIS, Carley's boyfriend

I was doing a physiology course online. Carley hated it because it took time that I could have spent with her. I went to the cottage a couple weekends in the summer. I was starting to realize I fell in love with her more every day, and I didn't know how large my emotions for her could become. My love seemed limitless.

Our families went to Punta Cana together. They were always joking about it being a surprise wedding for Carley and me, and every time they would mention that, we would look at each other and know that it was the only thing we wanted: to get married.

We rented dune buggies. I was pretty cautious. But I was driving — somewhat adventurous for me. And Carley said, "Oh, we're, like, halfway there. Can I drive?"

I'm like, "Yeah, of course."

I didn't care — I could've sat for the whole time. But Carley drives like a freaking maniac. I thought the dune buggy was going to break, 'cause they're not the best built and she was taking me up and down dunes. I thought I was going to die. It was hilarious.

Then after that, we jumped in a cave, into water, to swim. May, Carley's mom, was very, very scared of that because everyone was just jumping into one spot. It was insane.

But Carley liked it. Anything that was crazy, adventurous stuff like that, she loved.

I am so thankful to have you in my life ♥

CARLEY'S BLOG

Ride to Conquer Cancer + CT Scan
Posted on August 24, 2014

Hey everyone!

It's almost time to start fundraising for next year's Ride to Conquer Cancer! This year we have developed a team called "Carley's Angel's"! Anyone who would like to ride with our team is welcome! All you have to do is sign up for the ride under the team name! We already have eight members, including me!

It's such a wonderful feeling to be healthy enough to participate in this year's ride. Princess Margaret has done so much for my family and me, and I cannot wait to give back to the place that gave me the opportunity to live a normal life again.

As for my health! I had a CT scan two weeks ago and we will get the results on Tuesday! My TSH (thyroid hormone) is finally in the normal range!! So excited to be moving forward!

Next weekend, I will be off to school, and it is such an unbelievable feeling. To think at this time last year, I was watching all of my friends go off to University while I was preparing for radiation. I am in a much better place now and I am so thankful for everything that has happened to me and my

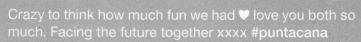

Crazy to think how much fun we had ♥ love you both so much. Facing the future together xxxx #puntacana

family. At this time last year the finish line seemed so far away, yet now I'm looking back on it feeling proud that I got through it and am starting a new life.

For the longest time, I wished for things to go back to normal but I came to realize that nothing will ever be the same and "normal" was something I could no longer comprehend. Just like when I was going through the transition from being a Grade Twelve student to going to Chemo, I am looking for a "new" normal. I'm sure it will take me some time to find it, but I know I'll have a great time looking for it.

I will keep everyone updated with the results of the scan! Lots of love to you all!

xo
Carley

CHAPTER NINE

Even in the darkest days,
it is a beautiful life.
— Carley

MARK ALLISON, Carley's dad

At the time, we were going through the scans, and they told us they were going to scan her January of 2014 and were going to do four scans, and if she made it through four, the chances of the cancer metastasizing went down exponentially.

So, we had had two scans, and in fact we had the third one when we went to Punta Cana. We just didn't have the results.

They had shown us spots in her lungs with the first two scans, but they said they'd always been there. But by the time of the third scan there were fifty spots. It was a huge amount of disease. The doctor just told us right out. She said, "She's going to die." We said, "We're not going there," but the doctor wanted to tell Carley. We didn't want that.

The doctor told us two years, so we thought, Okay, at least until Christmas she could be at university, taking these pills and leading a normal life. We'd just had an amazing summer — Carley looked amazing; she was running on the beach; she was playing volleyball; she didn't complain to me that she was a little bit sore — and when your lung has cancer in it, you can get soreness in places.

Carley wanted to go to university. She could take pills, and she should be able to function okay.

Carley wanted to go live.

MARK, MAY, RILEY and SAMANTHA ALLISON, Carley's family

MARK: May received the phone call at work.

MAY: The doctor asked me if I was sitting down, and then she told me over the phone. She said, "Carley's cancer has spread to her lungs."

My first question was "What does that mean?"

She said, "We could try to treat it with chemotherapy drugs."

I asked, "How long?"

She said, "Well, you know, first drug probably will last about eight months, and then we can try another drug."

And I said, "Well, how long does she have?"

She said, "Two years." I remember that day so clearly because Cheryl, one of the girls I work with, and I were doing an ALS — amyotrophic lateral sclerosis — Challenge.

SAMANTHA: Yeah, the Ice Bucket Challenge.

MAY: Where everyone was dumping an ice bucket of water over their heads. So, we were doing one at work, dressed in our AutoPlanet stuff, and anyway, I remember just looking at Cheryl and not saying anything and leaving.

MARK: And so May came home, and Sammy and Carley were coming back from Starbucks?

SAMANTHA: Yeah.

MARK: When Carley got home, May and I went into her room. She was in her room alone, getting ready to go skating, and then we told her. And she literally just said, you know, "Okay." I don't think she — she didn't cry or anything. Did she, May?

RILEY: She did afterward.

MAY: Yeah.

SAMANTHA: Yeah, she did.

RILEY: But it was, like, only for two minutes.

MARK: Yeah, and then she went skating.

SAMANTHA ALLISON, Carley's sister

I got back from Starbucks and I was watching TV, and Dad turned off the TV.

He said, "I have to talk to you about something."

I said, "What's wrong?"

He started crying, and he said, "Carley's cancer has come back."

Honestly to God, I thought he was joking. I was, like, "Stop kidding around — that's not a funny joke. Don't do that to me."

He said, "I'm not kidding."

JOHN SERVINIS, Carley's boyfriend

Carley got rediagnosed with cancer in her lungs. She called me as soon as she found out. My parents sat down with me, saying it was not looking good for Carley.

I stared at them, saying, "No," thinking that they couldn't lose hope that easily. She could beat this.

I drove over to Carley's house and spent the afternoon and night with her. She asked me if I wanted to end our relationship.

I said, "No."

She asked, "Why not?"

I said, "Because I'm in love with you, and it's ridiculous to even think that."

Then she kissed me.

LYNDSAY REDDICK, Carley's friend

Two nights after Riley told us that Car had been diagnosed again, the Allison family had planned a joint birthday party for all their big birthdays. Sammy was sixteen, Carley was nineteen, Riley was twenty-one and May was fifty. The plan was to throw a huge birthday party in their backyard. They decided to go ahead with the party — Carley didn't want anyone to know about her diagnosis yet. My sister and I knew. Her parents and siblings knew. A couple of her friends knew. And John knew. The party was gorgeous — all the girls in the Allison family love to have a party. Any time May gets a chance, she has an event in the back-yard and puts up a big white tent. A family friend catered this party, and there were tables of food. Riley, Carley and Sammy loved to dress up, so they were all in dresses and heels. Everyone was dressed up — the guys were wearing nice clothes. It was really, really hot — everyone was sweating, and they had little gelato stations in the backyard. There was music playing.

We had this whole party, and it was for everyone's birthday, and we were hanging out and drinking, and Carley didn't want anyone to know. We put on a happy face for her because she didn't want anyone to be sad. She didn't want anyone to feel pity for her.

Toward the end of the party Riley, Jenny, Carley and I all went upstairs. I can't remember why. I can't remember what we were doing, and I think it was because we just wanted to talk, because that was the first time we had seen each other since finding out Car had been rediagnosed.

Car and I were lying in her bed, just chatting, and we were

holding hands, and then all of a sudden we both went silent.

I said, "Car, I'm really scared."

And she said, "Yeah. I'm really scared, too."

That's the only time through either of her diagnoses, any of her treatment that she ever told me she was worried or scared, and then from that moment on she just lived that positive attitude.

CARLEY'S BLOG

Unexpected CT Scan results
Posted on August 27, 2014

I met with my medical oncologist to discuss the results of my CT scan. I have been diagnosed with clear cell sarcoma in my lungs. My cancer has spread from my neck to my lungs. I will be taking a trial oral chemotherapy to stop the growth of the cancer in my lungs. It still feels surreal to me that my cancer is back, but I can't dwell on it now. It's time to fight again. I know it won't be easy but at least I know what I'm headed for this time. Thank you everyone for your continued support. My friends and family are the reason I'm able to stay so strong.

It's crazy to think just a few days ago I blogged about how I'm moving forward with my life. In a sense, I still am, there's just going to be a few more bumps in the road. I will still be off to university on Sunday, but I will be home often to see the doctors and check the progress of the chemotherapy pill. The side effects are similar to traditional chemo, but I will not lose my hair and I may not feel as sick. I am hoping I will be well enough to continue living my life the way I would like to.

As much as the news upset my family and me, we know exactly how to handle it.

"God will only give me as much as I can handle, I just wish he didn't trust me so much."

my best frannn ❤ I know the next steps won't be easy but at least I kinda know what to expect. Thank you everyone for your continued support. My friends and family are the reason I'm able to stay so strong

CHAPTER TEN

Live each day to the most, because life is not very long.
— Carley

CARLEY

I still don't look up and think, Oh, I have cancer. Is it trying to kill me? No, I don't think so. It's trying to teach me.

Surreal to think 5 days ago we were on vacation, and my biggest stress was getting ready for university. Cancer has no idea who it is dealing with #findacureforclearcellsarcoma #fuckcancer

CARLEY'S BLOG

Chemo 2.0
Posted on August 29, 2014

Today I started taking the chemotherapy pills. I only took them an hour ago so I haven't felt any side effects yet. It was a very strange feeling taking chemo from a bottle, in pill form. All day long I was looking over at the bottle trying to wrap my head around the fact that the bottle contained chemo. From my past experience chemo was administered in liquid IV form in the hospital, and my nurses had to wear gowns and a protective mask before hanging the bag on my IV tower. It was so strange to just be able to access the chemo at a time I chose, pour the pills into a little cup and swallow them. I still have to follow most of the same rules as before, like no grapefruit, Advil, mouthwash, and the weird list goes on and on but I basically have it memorized from last year. And that's the thing ... I never imagined having to use this knowledge again. Just like yesterday when my doctor asked me if I had any leftover anti-nausea medication, and lo and behold we had all the medication. It felt like I was back in March 2013 looking through all the chemo medications making sure I had enough before we started the next round.

I'm still trying to understand everything that is going on right now, and part of me thinks I haven't even come to terms with the fact my cancer is back. It does not feel real yet, but I know it will soon. Cancer tried to beat me once and it failed, and it will continue to fail. I know I can beat this, it will just take more time. God has a plan for me, and this is the journey he's taking me on to find it. I want to do great things with my life and I know one day I will be able to.

I will keep you all updated with treatment plans and how I am feeling.

I love you all.

SAMANTHA ALLISON, Carley's sister

I went in Carley's car with her to drive her to university, and my parents went in their car. Carley had a lot of stuff, so we had to take two cars.

We were talking about her rediagnosis. She was driving. She glanced at me and said, "It wouldn't have worked if this had happened to anyone else in the family, because you're too young, Riley's still at school and Mom and Dad — well, it couldn't have happened to them. It happened to me because I can handle it."

She talked about how cancer made us all stronger, and it made us all stronger as a family, and it made her appreciate so many more things than she had before.

CARLEY'S BLOG

24 Hours later ...
Posted on September 1, 2014

Yesterday at 3:00, my family and I were finished moving me into my room at Queen's, and they headed back to Toronto. Last night in the middle of the night I started feeling some pain in my chest. I woke up to go running and I could barely move, it was difficult even trying to get changed. I tried to go running, thinking maybe it would make me feel better. I took one step and I knew I wasn't going to be able to run. Chest pain is a side effect of the oral chemotherapy, and the sheet of side effects mentioned that if I develop severe chest pain, I need to go to the ER. I waited a bit to see if the pain was going away but it didn't. I called my sister's best friend (Natalie Beaton, my second sister) and she came to pick me up and take me to the ER. John also met us there a few minutes later.

We waited as I got a chest X-ray, and all my vitals checked. I thought that maybe I had some water in my lungs, but that wasn't the case. My parents came to Kingston to pick me up and take me to Toronto to see my doctors tomorrow. I will hopefully be back in Kingston on Wednesday.

It's very frustrating for me that I've only been in Kingston for 24 hours before I had an emergency. All I want is to be able to do the things I want to do. Running in the mornings makes me feel so relaxed and sets me up for a great day. I was upset that I could not run today and I had to come back to Toronto. I would love to just wake up tomorrow and not be in any pain, but I know that's not something realistic to ask for. It's just frustrating because I felt perfectly fine yesterday and all the days leading up to going to Kingston. I know in time everything will be okay, but right now it feels like my body just doesn't want to cooperate with me.

I'm praying for a brighter tomorrow.

♥

Crazy Week
Posted on September 11, 2014

It's officially been seven days that I've had a fever over 38°C. I stayed at Queen's until last Sunday morning when my fever reached over 40°C and I had to come home. I am thankfully back at school today but I will have to see how I am feeling. It's pretty frustrating that I have missed almost the entire first week of classes, but I know that shouldn't be my biggest worry right now.

Yesterday my parents and I went to the Dana-Farber Cancer Institute in Boston. I walked in and it looked like a hotel, so I asked my parents where we were 'cause it definitely didn't look like a hospital to me. We sat and waited for our appointment and this lady came up to us and gave me this little monitor, she said it was a tracking device so the doctor would know where I am at all times in the hospital. I thought it was a bit strange but I went along with it.

While speaking with the doctor in Boston, he said something that caught my attention. He explained chemo like it was a "bomb" and it's used to kill anything and everything inside of you to kill the cancer. I have never heard anyone explain it like that before. It made it seem like the healthy parts of my body were being destroyed in the process, but I guess that's true. They have to almost kill you to save your life. But this is all different to the chemo I'm on now. The chemo I am on now is a targeted therapy and is not doing as much damage to my healthy cells as traditional chemotherapy, which is probably why I wasn't feeling the same effects as the last time I had chemo.

Finally, our long day of appointments ended and we were on our way back to the airport. I was very relieved to be coming home since I was still very sick.

It's pretty weird realizing that I am at school and I am battling cancer at the same time. It's life and I have to enjoy it as it is. Cancer sucks but it would suck even more if I let the cancer take over my life.

It's been a rough couple of weeks since I got this cold and

fever but things are starting to look better. My fever has gone down a lot and my energy levels are improving. I just can't wait to wake up one day and feel completely healthy. I know it was only four weeks ago I was feeling great but it feels like a lifetime ago.

Thank you everyone for all your love ♥

♥

Back home!
Posted on September 16, 2014

Last night I came home from Kingston for a doctor's appointment this morning. The appointment was with our oncologist to assess my fever and cold. I have been feeling much better over the last few days but I still do not feel great. We started the chemo again on Sunday night so that could be the reason I'm starting to feel not so great again.

These days I find there's no way to describe how I feel. I get upset about everything and just feel like crying but then I look at the big picture and I realize this is just going to be another battle I'm going to win. It's going to be another trophy to put up on the mantel. "Conquered cancer, Round 2." I know those words are far from being said but I do know there will be a time when I say them. It's not going to be an easy fight, and I can't say I'd be able to do it alone, but with the help of my friends and family I know it's possible.

xoxo
Carley

♥

Getting things under control!
Posted on September 20, 2014

Today I met with an academic advisor to talk about my options regarding courses, since I have already, and will be missing lots of school. We decided the best option for me would be to put my courses online. I can still go to class if I am at school but if I am away there will be no penalty for my absence. I'm very excited that things are being worked out and I can have the flexibility to be home if I need to be. As for how I am feeling ... I have been okay these days. I struggle in the mornings to get out of bed, and sleeping is sometimes a challenge, but for the most part I'm pretty good during the day! Last night in the middle of the night I was a bit nauseous and I was having some trouble getting comfortable but I took my anti-nausea medication and I felt much better. Some days when I'm at school I forget that I am sick. I wake up feeling not so good but then it goes away and I move on with my day. In some ways I can act just like any other normal student during the day. But when the clock turns to 9:00 p.m., I get the notification on my phone to take my chemo, that's when it hits me. It's such a strange feeling. I will be at dinner with my friends or hanging out with my friends and I have to go back to my room for a few minutes to take the chemo. It's just not something I ever imagined myself going through.

But as I've said before, this is the situation and we need to deal with it head on. It doesn't matter what it takes I know I will be better soon. It's just a matter of time.

I will soon be having a needle biopsy to get a sample of the larger tumor pressing against my rib (which is not as painful anymore so I'm hoping it's the medication working!!!) I will keep everyone updated with the results.

Love,
Carley ♥

SAMANTHA ALLISON, Carley's sister

She had to come back from university — she was too sick to stay. And I remember that one day Sarah was supposed to come over, and Sarah said, "Carley, I have a cold. I can't come over."

Carley was dealing with her new chemo. She was super sick, and Carley said, "Oh, my God, Sarah, I don't care if you can't come over. But are you okay? Do you need me to bring you coffee?"

Sarah was, like, "Are you kidding me right now? I have a cold. You're in chemo."

SARAH FISHER, Carley's friend

Carley came back from university after just a few weeks. I was home that year, and so we spent a lot of time together. She and I went to Menchie's a lot. Car would just pile so much on her yogurt. They should be about seven dollars, but our frozen yogurts would end up at twelve dollars when we went because we'd put so much on. Then the yogurts would melt and become this pool of candy, and it was disgusting. But the place was fabulous, and we mostly went there. We loved going there. But I'd usually come to Car's house. She wasn't always feeling great. When we were at her house, we'd just lie on her couch and catch up and talk.

love this girl to the moon

MICHAEL NADEL, family friend

In September of 2014, Carley was showing progress and was strong enough to sing the national anthem at the Princess Margaret Cancer Foundation's Road Hockey to Conquer Cancer. It was an extremely moving rendition, as Carley toughed through it despite the obvious pain and difficulty she was experiencing with her reconstructed trachea. In the midst of the anthem, Carley had to stop to catch her breath, rest her vocal cords for a moment, and then she valiantly finished to a rousing standing ovation that felt like it went on forever. Former Team Canada legend Paul Henderson, a Canadian icon, who spoke just after Carley sang the anthem, was visibly overwhelmed, as were all those in attendance. He focused his speech on Carley Allison and said something to the effect of "Well, what can I say? This is clearly the Carley Allison show ... what else can I say?" Such was the sentiment of all the great speakers during this memorable and moving event; Carley's grit and determination to get through the anthem captured everyone's hearts and inspired us in a way only Carley could.

Carley's father, Mark, and I shared concern over the fact that Carley was scheduled to sing the national anthem at the Air Canada Centre the very next day, September 28, 2014, for an NHL preseason game between the Toronto Maple Leafs and the Buffalo Sabres. I had organized it, but she was growing weaker. The concern was that without having a proper introduction, the audience might not understand why Carley's rendition of the anthem was the way it was. I had requested MLSE —Maple Leaf Sports and Entertainment — to make a special announcement, but MLSE advised that the hockey club had a mere three minutes to introduce the two singers and have them perform both national anthems. Failure to do so could result in a fine of $10,000 levied by the NHL against the hockey club.

I haven't had the chance to thank my amazing family and friends who came out to the game! It felt great knowing I had all your support ♥ ♥ so grateful to be a part of this #fuckcancer

As providence would be, Larry Tanenbaum, the chairman of MLSE, was in attendance at the Princess Margaret Hospital Road Hockey to Conquer Cancer event. I confronted Tanenbaum and said, "Mr. Tanenbaum, I need to talk to you about Carley Allison." Mr. Tanenbaum, who had arrived after Carley's anthem performance, said he'd heard that Carley was a great singer and suggested that she sing at the Air Canada Centre, to which I replied, "Well, sir, she is … tomorrow … That's why we need to talk."

I explained the difficulty Carley had singing the anthem and the need for a brief introduction to provide some context for her performance. I acknowledged his sensitivity to the time limitation and the associated financial penalty thereof and assured Mr. Tanenbaum that he and longtime friend Andy Frost, the ACC public address announcer, could develop a short announcement, economic in words, to properly set the stage for Carley. Mr. Tanenbaum gave me his blessing, and the following announcement was made by Andy Frost prior to Carley's singing of the anthem:

"WILL YOU PLEASE REMAIN STANDING AND WELCOME OUR SINGER FOR TONIGHT'S CANADIAN NATIONAL ANTHEM. SHE WAS DIAGNOSED WITH AN EXTREMELY RARE TRACHEA CANCER IN 2013 AND IS NOW FIGHTING DOUBLE LUNG CANCER, BUT THAT HAS NOT STOPPED HER FROM PERFORMING FOR US TONIGHT. PLEASE JOIN ME IN WELCOMING CARLEY ALLISON."

Carley's performance was spot-on. Her voice was gentle yet powerful, and her emotion was undeniable. Mark, May and everyone else were absolutely ecstatic, and most important, Carley, who had extremely high standards, was pleased with her performance. It was night and day when compared with the performance the day before at the Road Hockey to Conquer Cancer event. This may have been due in small part to the fact that Carley acknowledged it was the first time in a long time that she woke up "with a voice." I was concerned about Carley's throat because of the performance the prior day and brought Carley some Throat Coat teabags, which helped soothe Carley's throat for her performance at the Air Canada Centre that day.

Due to her strong performance, she was invited to sing the anthem again on November 1, 2014, for the NHL's Hockey Fights Cancer match, with the Toronto Maple Leafs taking on the Chicago Blackhawks.

CARLEY'S BLOG

Leafs game!
Posted on September 29, 2014

Had an amazing time tonight at the game! Sang the Canadian anthem and got to hang out with Dion Phaneuf. He showed us the dressing room. And gave us all jerseys with our name on the back, all of us Allisons!

♥

Road Hockey to Conquer Cancer
Posted on October 1, 2014

This past Saturday, I sang the national anthem for the PMH Road Hockey to Conquer Cancer tournament. It was so incredible to be sharing the stage with so many hockey legends, while being able to perform the national anthem to kick off the event.

Thank you very much to Paul Alofs for your kind words today on your blog!

Last Saturday, the Princess Margaret Cancer Foundation hosted the 4th Annual Road Hockey to Conquer Cancer. It was a phenomenal success with

1,387 players who formed 122 teams and raised a remarkable $2,219,000. At the opening ceremony, Mr. Hockey, Paul Henderson, spoke about his courageous battle with cancer. The absolute highlight of the opening ceremony was when Carley Allison sang the Canadian national anthem. Carley was diagnosed in 2013 with an extremely rare sarcoma near her trachea. She was successfully treated by Dr. Pat Gullane, one of the world's great head and neck cancer surgeons and the leader here at Princess Margaret. We also heard that Carley's cancer had returned, this time in her lungs. This incredibly courageous and inspirational first-year university student stood in front of a hushed crowd and sang a brilliant version of "O Canada."

Courage is something we all talk about but it's often difficult to define. To me, I saw the definition of courage in the face of Carley Allison and heard the voice of courage as she sang. Carley has an incredible family and circle of supporters who bring their passion and commitment to her treatment ... Courage, passion, and inspiration together in one very exceptional young lady.

Thanks, Carley, from all of us!

CARLEY

I'm in my favorite room by the kitchen — just a few short weeks ago, I thought everything would be so different. But right now, I'm appreciating the sunlight through the window. And the way this room always smells good, of flowers and of shea body lotion. The body lotion is me. The flowers are from Mom. And the smell of cooking comes in from the kitchen — today Mom is making something with chicken and spices for a big family supper — we're having Dad's side of the family over — his brothers, their wives, my cousins. I can't wait to see my cousin Jeff, especially, today. Sometimes I'm just in the mood to be with him. The smell coming from the kitchen reminds me of my grandmother, of Joni, when she used to cook, and that doesn't help my fatigue. I feel sad suddenly, as I miss her — although I'm glad she never lived to see me like this. Tears well in my eyes, and I rub them away before they can fall. I think today I'm worn down because I have another cold, and it just feels like one thing too much. I suppose the radiation I've started isn't making me feel any better either. Urgh. A little cold, starting radiation, and I'm a pussycat curled up on the couch.

I imagine what it would be like to have a dog curled up next to me — our dog, Jack, isn't much of a cuddler. I yawn. Maybe I'll have a bit of a sleep. I'll dream of what my life is like when I get over this — I imagine myself working my way up through Mom's dealership. I can see myself, maybe if I work hard, running the place. I think I'd be a good manager — and I love working with cars. I imagine a long day at work after we've sold a lot of cars. I go home to my house, where John is just home, too, from his dentistry practice. Maybe he owns one up near the Dairy Queen and that beautiful view. We talk about his job, about the people and their teeth. I tell him we sold a lot of cars, and we decide not to bother cooking. Not tonight. We're going to go for supper at a Greek restaurant. Maybe an old favorite like Mezes, on the Danforth. Perhaps we'll meet his mom there and tell her the news — in this fantasy I'm pregnant. With twins. A boy and a girl. We'll watch the waiter bring over a flaming dish of fried cheese, and I'll tuck in. I know, I know, not the healthiest dish, but my body will be feeding me and the babies, so I'll eat a load of it.

Even lying here, thinking about this, I'm pretty sure I feel a bit better. This is only a cold. And there's no way cancer is going to take away all these dreams. No way.

I call out to Mom, "After I've had a nap, I'm going to come and help you."

She leans her head around the doorway. Her dark hair frames her worried face. "If you're sure you're up to it. We could always cancel tonight, Carley — we could just have a quiet evening if you're not feeling well."

"I'm fine. It's just a cold. But I was thinking, maybe I need a dog for days like this."

"No!" She laughs. "We have a dog."

"How about I do a little research into another dog?"

"No. More. Dogs. No." She shakes her head, smiles and disappears back into the kitchen.

I don't think that was a definite no. Perhaps before I nap, I'll do a bit more research into getting a puppy.

CARLEY'S BLOG

Hey everyone!
Posted on October 21, 2014

Sorry I haven't posted in a long time. I haven't been feeling so well. Last week was not a good week for me, I barely got out of bed. Things are starting to get better and I am starting to come out of this "radiation funk." I'm not going to say this past week has been easy and that I just toughed through and I'm okay. But I will say that I did it! I completed the five days of extremely high intensity radiation and it's OVER!

I am so happy to have completed one step of the road to recovery though we don't exactly know what the rest of the road entails. For now I am back on the chemotherapy pills and I am meeting with my oncologist today to see how well it's working.

Lots of exciting things coming up! This Friday (October 24th), the Queen's men's hockey team has organized for the game against Guelph to be used to raise money and awareness for the Princess Margaret Foundation. I will also be singing the national anthem at the game!

Also! On November 1st, I will be singing the National Anthem at the ACC! I am extremely excited since I got all the nerves out in the pre season game!

The effects of the chemo and radiation have been much different than last time I was treated. My radiation this time around was very close to my stomach so nausea has been my biggest issue. We have been trying to learn lots of natural remedies to control the nausea since the medication doesn't always do the trick. The chemo, on the other hand, has some really strange side effects. I am not losing my hair but it is changing color! The roots of my hair have turned white. It looks a bit weird but it's much better than losing my hair! I did pull my wigs out the other day though just for old times sake, and I have to say I look like a completely different person with my wig on! I completely forgot what I look like with long hair. It was definitely an emotional experience, but short hair is the least of my problems.

I should be thankful to at least have hair, but sometimes it's hard.

♥

Puck Cancer
Posted on October 25, 2014

Yesterday was an amazing day! For one it was amazing because I woke up and felt good!! But yesterday was amazing mostly because it was the PUCK CANCER event! The Queen's men's hockey team played an amazing game, beating Guelph 3-2. So many people came out to the game it was incredible! It was such an amazing feeling to see people I didn't even know helping out and volunteering. A big thank you to Braeden who was the main drive behind the operation! He did such an amazing job organizing everything — I cannot thank him enough. I sang the national anthem at the beginning of the game and I have to say, I think I was less nervous at the ACC. I was just about to sing in front of family, friends and my fellow Gaels ... yet I was so nervous. The event tonight really meant a lot to me and I felt like I needed to do the team justice!

All and all the event went great! We will soon know an estimate of how much money we raised. And it definitely didn't hurt that HILARY DUFF donated $500.00!

Thanks again to everyone who came out last night!!

Here's the National Anthem. Let me know what you think!

VIDEO: Puck Cancer — National Anthem by Carley Elle Allison
www.youtube.com/watch?v=xE5l17nlNsk

MARK ALLISON, Carley's dad

Carley was pumped to sing the national anthem again on November 1, Saturday night, right across Canada, for Hockey Fights Cancer. And thanks to Michael Nadel, MLSE did a little announcement beforehand to disclose her cancer. And so Carley sang in the Air Canada Centre, and she did a wonderful job, and it was in Toronto and the Leafs won. Carley was fabulous, and it was a live broadcast across Canada because the game was on *Hockey Night in Canada*. Millions of people watched her sing. Michael told me that he'll always remember walking through the ACC with Carley after her performance. She couldn't go two feet before having someone else come up to her glowing with praise. Carley not only nailed the anthem, she owned it. It was sung in a way only Carley could, with so much passion, love, determination and emotion, and with a reconstructed throat and with double lung cancer.

Carley was taking her chemo pills, and she wasn't feeling good, but she got herself up for that performance. Then she just started watching the game with John, Riley and Riley's boyfriend.

They stayed that night at a nice hotel near the Air Canada Centre. And the next morning they had to get home at six in the morning so that Carley could go to Hippocrates — a center in Florida where they work with alternative therapies.

On her way home from the hotel, she told me she threw up in the car. She was always sick.

LYNDSAY REDDICK, Carley's friend

Carley had been upset during the fall. She really wanted to have the university experience after all her friends had been there the year before, and she really wanted to be close to John, and she really liked school, and she was meeting lots of people there. So, she was really, really upset that she couldn't be there, and she still tried to stay positive and exercise and do the things that she enjoyed, but I think that really took a toll on her state of mind. And it also took a toll because the doctors were telling her there was nothing she could do, and she was trying everything, and she of course refused to admit that that was even a possibility — that there was nothing they could do. So, she was fighting her own battle while dealing with the medical system giving up on her. That's how she felt and how we felt, and what her family felt is that the doctors just gave up on her.

Her family took her to a natural wellness facility in Florida, and that's when we all knew that this was her last option. I remember her dad saying, "After this everyone is saying there's nothing we can do, there's limited time. There are trial drugs in other countries, but Carley is going to run out of time before we can get her on those tests and trials." That's when I really knew that this was not going well.

CARLEY'S BLOG

Hippocrates

Posted on November 4, 2014

battling cancer the natural way #lovemesomegreens #beatingtheodds

Yesterday I landed in Florida to start my journey on becoming raw vegan and killing my cancer!! My mom and I are participating in a three-week program at Hippocrates. Hippocrates is an institution where people go to improve their health with a raw vegan diet. The diet consists of vegetables and sprouts, juiced vegetables and wheat grass. Since I got to Hippocrates institute I have been blown away. The atmosphere here and all the people here are so positive that it's incredible. Everyone here is going through some sort of health related complication and it's amazing to see so many people motivated to change their lives.

I will say, though, it hasn't been easy since I got here. The change in diet along with the wheat grass juice, has been pretty hard on me. But I have been told that after a week or so it gets much better, so I'm just looking forward to that!

I will keep everyone updated on my and my mom's progress here in Florida!

Xoxo
Carley

♥

Bright days ahead
Posted on November 8, 2014

I have not had the easiest of weeks. When I got to Hippocrates, I was motivated to embrace the new lifestyle, but I didn't understand what it actually entails until I started having problems. Earlier this week, I wasn't able to get out of bed, and today I spent the entire day up and about!

I watched the graduation of the session earlier than mine and it was incredible. Every single person graduating walked onto the stage and spoke about their experiences here, and the amount of people that say they feel better, their pain is gone, their TUMOR shrunk it's just amazing. When I first got here, I didn't know if I would be able to do this. I felt sick, I couldn't get out of bed, and I had to go to the hospital because one night I just got too sick. But between today and yesterday I feel like I'm starting to see the light.

I am so confident with what I am doing and I know when I get my next scan results we WILL see positive changes.

Xoxo

JOHN SERVINIS, Carley's boyfriend

I visited her in Florida at Hippocrates, which was coincidentally on our one-year-and-six-month anniversary. I got her a silver necklace and bracelet. It was the first time I danced with her. It was a basic salsa. I could feel the love she had for me as she looked in my eyes.

After spending the day at Hippocrates, Mark, Sammy, Riley and I got into the car. Mark and I looked at each other and unanimously decided to go to Wendy's to grab a couple burgers. That day I really respected Carley as she pushed her limits mentally and physically. She was there living a raw vegan diet; meanwhile, I could barely even last a full day of it.

CARLEY'S BLOG

Interesting Week
Posted on November 16, 2014

This past week here at Hippocrates has been very interesting. It started off pretty well. I was up and doing things every day and really taking advantage of my time here. But then I ran into a problem. I started to feel really sick. I couldn't even find the energy to get myself out of bed. Eventually Thursday came and I hit an ultimate low. I was in bed in extreme discomfort from nausea and my mom wasn't sure if there was anything else she could do to make me feel better. Finally, we called the health care team and we decided to take me to the hospital. The moment they gave me anti-nausea medication I was good to go. I felt so much better it was insane. After two liters of IV fluids, they sent me home, and since then I have been feeling great! I think I really just needed to get the nausea under control so that I can participate in everyday activities.

Now that I am feeling better I am ready to start my final week here and enjoy every moment of it. I feel so grateful to be able to go on this journey to cure myself and continue this healthy lifestyle. I will let you all know how the week goes. I can't believe I have already reached my last week of this journey. It hasn't been easy but I know I have gotten through the hardest part. Today I finally had enough energy to go to the gym! I didn't do much other than stretching and some yoga, but it's a start, right?

Tomorrow, I will have blood taken for the first time since I've been here and I am really excited to see what they find! I know everything is going to look just perfect! This past weekend my family and boyfriend came to visit my mom and me! I don't know how to express how happy I was to see them. Being in this institution you begin to feel pretty isolated, so to be able to spend time with people in the "real world" felt amazing! We went out shopping and went to a delicious vegan restaurant! I don't mind eating the raw vegan diet they have us on here, but it was really nice to have some new variety (that was still vegan) other than the same buffet we get here every day.

Lots of love to everyone! XO

♥

Leafs VS Chicago
Posted (same day) on November 16, 2014

Soooo, I realized I never made a blog about the Saturday night NHL game I got to sing at! I'm pretty much at a loss for words every time someone asks me what it was like, because I couldn't explain it at all, it was just so incredible. As a singer, having the entire ACC cheer for you is something you only dream of. Yet this year I got to experience it twice

AND got to sing on Hockey Night in Canada! Now my entire life I have watched Hockey Night in Canada on Saturday nights with my dad. I never imagined that it would be me singing that anthem on that TV.

It was nice to have a feeling of accomplishment from singing the anthem, since these days I've been feeling a bit useless. But I know that soon enough I will be healthy enough to start doing the things that make me feel better.

Love you all xoxo

♥

A Good Day!
Posted on November 17, 2014

Today started off a bit different than most days. I had to wake up before eight (I know, so early) to have blood taken to see if I'm able to have some vitamin C through IV. It was weird setting my alarm because for the last couple months I have been able to just wake up whenever I feel okay enough to wake up. But I set my alarm and got to the medical building for the blood work. It took about five minutes, and I walked back to my room and went right back to bed.

I woke up again around 10 feeling great. Since then I've

had a massage, gone for a swim and now my mom and I are sitting having some more sprouts, leafs, and vegetables for lunch! Later today, I will try to make it back to the gym. I know it really sounds like I'm living the life down here in Florida, but it definitely wasn't this peachy for the past two weeks. Now that I'm feeling better, I am able to finally participate in all the activities.

I want to say a huge thank you to all the people here that helped my mom and me through the first couple weeks. You guys made everything you could so much easier for me and I cannot thank you enough for taking us under your wing! I have been enjoying all different types of treatment thanks to the gift card you guys bought me. I am so overwhelmed by all the people here that just want to help.

I hope everyone back home in Toronto is keeping warm and enjoying the snow!

XO

♥

Awesome Quote
Posted on November 18, 2014

My mom bought me a shirt from the store here a few days

ago, and the message on the inside of the shirt was amazing!

"Strong Women: may we know them, may we raise them, may we be them."

♥

Be the Cancer
Posted on November 19, 2014

Today I had an appointment with the therapist here at HHI. Everyone here has two complimentary appointments with the therapist, and today I had my second session. We started off talking about nonsense, then got into how I was feeling since I've been here. I was very honest with him and I explained that my first two weeks were not easy. The time went on talking about my time here and finally he stopped me and said, "I'm going to switch gears for a minute, close your eyes and pretend you are the cancer." He added, "Tell me about yourself."

I closed my eyes and sat there for a minute. I didn't really know what to say. I had never really pictured myself as the cancer, nor did I have any idea what the cancer would say. I started off by saying, "Well, I kinda suck."

He responded, "Why?"

I said, "Because I'm trying to attack Carley."

He asked, "Do you think you'll win?"

I said, "Well I've tried before and I didn't, so why would I win this time."

He continued asking me questions until I came to the point where (still speaking as the cancer) I said, "I don't want to hurt Carley."

He responded with, "But you are."

I didn't know what to say for a minute since I knew I was completely contradicting myself. I suddenly realized that in my mind I believe the cancer inside of me isn't trying to kill me. I know it's there, I can feel it and the scans show it, but is it trying to kill me? No, I don't think so. It's trying to teach me. I used to think my body just wasn't cooperating with me and inhibiting me from doing the things I want to do. I'm realizing now that yes the cancer is preventing me from leading a "normal" teenage life.

But it's not trying to kill me.

I have learned so much through these past two years dealing with cancer. But do I wish I was at school? Yes! Do I wish I could still be training every day? Absolutely! But I wouldn't trade what I have learned in these past two years for anything. I'm not saying I wanted to have cancer or I like having cancer. But it has shown me so much and taught me so much I refuse to believe the cancer inside of me is a killer. It's more like a very difficult teacher that doesn't think I'm ready to graduate, but when it does, I will be the best version of myself possible.

♥

Home soon!
Posted on November 19, 2014

Coming home in three days!! I am so excited to be coming home to my family and friends in a few days! But I will be sad to leave this place (and I wouldn't have said that at this time last week). I am starting to feel so much better these days! Almost "normal" or whatever normal means right?

I'm not going to lie and say "oh everything was amazing and I had the most amazing three weeks of my life and I'm cancer free." No, that's not how this works. It was hard and I really had to push myself to adapt to this lifestyle. I felt sick, I was nauseous, and I just wanted to eat something comforting. But I pushed through those weeks with temptation and now … I still have temptation … but WAY less than the first two weeks.

Going home is very exciting, but also a bit daunting. Here,

we are given every meal, our juice is juiced fresh for us, and our wheat grass is grown for us.

At home I will have to start doing all of these things on my own and I know it is not going to be easy. My dad has already started growing us the wheat grass at home so I know with the help of my family this is all going to be possible. I also want to thank my mom for sticking by my side this entire time. I know this process wasn't easy for her either but she didn't complain and she did everything she could to make this as easy as possible for me.

♥

Instagram! "Dying to be me"
Posted on November 20, 2014

Hey everyone!

I have created an Instagram account to record my journey and raise awareness toward cancer! It's called "dyingtobeme." I just started it so there's not much to it but if anyone has Instagram and wants to follow go right ahead! The name came to me one day and I think it fits perfectly since I'm just dying to be myself again!

Love you all!

RILEY ALLISON, Carley's sister

We hated the name "dyingtobeme," but Carley loved it. She thought it was perfect. That was just what she was like — she had this sense of humor, and she just … she wanted to inspire people, even if she didn't always feel so brave.

CARLEY'S BLOG

Graduation
Posted on November 22, 2014

Today was finally our graduation! It was so inspiring to watch everyone get onstage and speak about their experiences here at Hippocrates! One woman got onstage and was speaking very highly of her experience and how it has helped her deal with the health complications of aging. Then she stopped and said, "I would like to specially thank one specific staff member that has made my time here incredible." She started telling us a story about when she was six and she didn't know how to swim. Her mother told her she couldn't go in the pool with her friends because she didn't know how to swim. Regardless of what her mom said, she went into the pool. She couldn't stay afloat and she went under, almost drowning. She is now 65 and has never been in the water since. Her husband was determined to teach her how to swim when they got married, but with countless attempts she just couldn't bring herself to get in the water. When she got to Hippocrates she saw on the itinerary that they offer swimming lessons. She said, "Well, I am in the Life Transformation Program! It's now or never!" So she signed herself up for some swimming lessons.

The instructor held her hand and brought her into the water, and within that one lesson she could fully submerge her ENTIRE body including her head under the water. It just goes to show that so many amazing things happen here every day! Her story inspired me that anything can happen!

Finally, it came to my mom's and my turn to go onstage and speak about our experience. I started off by telling the shortest version of my cancer journey I could, and then I spoke about one moment I had here that changed everything. I told everyone about my first week here. I was very sick and not really able to participate in the program. A group of adults that I had met earlier that day had gone out, bought me a card and a gift card that I could use anywhere here like the spa and salon! I was so overwhelmed by how many people came together and pitched in to buy me this gift card just to make me feel better.

When my mom and I were done speaking I went over to the piano to play a song to end the graduation. I sang the song I wrote about my previous cancer experience! It was really nice sharing that song with so many people that are dealing with a similar health problem. I can't believe that three weeks have gone by but I cannot wait to get home and get things all ready for Christmas (the best holiday)!

♥

Some Sort of Incredible

Posted on November 23, 2014

Throughout my time in Florida I learned a lot. From attending lectures, to meeting so many amazing people from all over the world, I have also learned a tremendous amount about myself.

I feel like I have finally come to terms with the fact that I am sick again. When I was rediagnosed in August, I tried to push it away. I went off to university thinking I could live a perfectly normal teenage life, and continue my education while on the chemotherapy. I found that I just became too sick to be at school, I dropped my classes and came home. I spent my days on the couch at home unable to do much other than sleep and eat a little. My spirits were definitely down and I wasn't feeling like myself. I feel like I finally am at a place where I accept the fact that I have cancer again and now it's time to do everything in my power to get better. I will most likely be home for the remainder of the school year, which used to really upset me but my life is so much more important than school or a party or pasta or a choco-late cake or anything that only provides instant satisfaction because I know it will only hurt me in the end. I need to put all my energy into kicking this cancer to the curb once and for all. School will be waiting for me when I'm ready and so will the parties, my pasta and chocolate cake, but for now it's just not worth it.

Regardless of what any doctor or anyone says, I know that I am going to live an amazing fulfilled life; I was just forced to grow up a little too fast. But hey, who says I can't be nineteen when I'm twenty-five right? I hate when I beat myself up about missing out on nineteen-year-old things, but I figure I have all the time in the world to do those things! I can be nineteen whenever I want.

I'm not saying I don't get upset though and I never have moments of grief. But I can honestly say I have never wished for a different life. I live a beautiful life.

CHAPTER ELEVEN

I've never been stronger
than I am right now.
— Carley

JOHN SERVINIS, Carley's boyfriend

The odds were looking pretty slim for what they were willing to give Carley. She'd always try to break up with me. I said, "Carley, I don't want to break up with you. I know what I want. I've known for a very long time what I want."

She'd always say, like, "You're at university. There're so many pretty girls there. You could have a grown-up life."

And I'm, like, "That's not what I want."

I surprised Carley by showing up at the last skating competition she competed in. She hated that I surprised her, but she loved seeing me there. She wouldn't ever admit that. I made her nervous that day, especially, but she loved me being there. We had a connection where no one could ever tell how we felt except the two of us. Carley was very open about her emotions and often didn't hide them, but Carley knew I hid all of mine. When I would smile, she could tell if it was with anger, sadness or any emotion. She was the only person to know how I felt about anything.

SHIN AMANO, Carley's skating coach

That day [November 28, 2014], she was just skating on her own, no jumping, and she was just happy to see everyone, and I didn't know how bad her condition was, but she said, "Next year when I feel good, I will try to skate, but today I just have to be careful." She said, "Hopefully, I can skate after New Year's." But after New Year's I didn't hear from her for a long time. She always wanted to be a champion; she wanted to be better than other skaters. She got mad at herself all the time, and it's not because she thought, That's so hard for me.

She just wanted to be her best.

HOLLY DE JONGE, family friend

Carley really wanted a breed of dog called a Pomsky. Carley and I never got into any arguments, but I was against the whole idea of designer breeds like Pomskys, and I tried to get her to get a different type of dog. But Carley didn't like that — she had her heart set on this dog, and she got really mad at me. Anyway, she got the dog she wanted, and I'm so happy that she did, because I think that dog was really like her therapy dog. It gave her something to love and to care for, and she really needed that at that time.

JOHN SERVINIS, Carley's boyfriend

We bought Tobi in December. We had to go to the airport because Tobi came from Calgary. There's a place around the back of Toronto airport where you can pick up large packages. So, we drove — well, she drove — to the airport. She's like, "John, let's go get our baby, like right now."

Carley is beyond excited. We get there, and the dog's in the back, and Carley had signed all her paperwork. Carley's shaking. She sees Tobi in her crate, and she opens it, and Tobi jumps in her arms. And she wouldn't let me touch Tobi at all. It was like she had to let Tobi imprint on her. She said, "John, stay away. You can't even look at her."

I said, "Oh, my God. I'm, like, the dog's not even — she won't imprint on me at all. Like, she's going to know she's your — that you're her mom."

Carley goes, "No, you can't risk it. Like, you can't be that dad. You can't be the on-and-off dad."

We were about to go home, and Carley's about to drive, and I'm holding Tobi, which is already a huge problem.

She's, like, "John, you can't hold Tobi. She's going to imprint with you faster than she will with me. She's going to know your scent."

"Jesus Christ, Carley, like, it's a dog. Like, it's not going to do this stuff. Like, I promise you this dog will love you way more than anyone else," I said.

She's like, "No, I can't do this. You have to drive."

I'm like, "Carley, you're already driving. We're almost on the highway."

She said, "I can't do this."

I'm like, "Okay, fine. You can do whatever you want." So, we're on the ramp to go on the highway, and it's very dark at this point, and we stop to switch seats. Carley and Tobi, they're, like, huddling together — and I just drove off. I swear Carley almost cried ten times that day alone. It was ridiculous. And cute. So cute.

Everyone made fun of us, saying Tobi was our baby and our first child together; the parents joined in by saying they were grandparents. But it felt like we had made our family. Not any sort of conventional family, but it was Carley, Tobi and me.

LYNDSAY REDDICK, Carley's friend

There's a Christmas Market in the Distillery District every year. So, Car and I and our older sisters went, and Car brought Tobi. We just walked around the market and hung out, and then we went to sit in the back of her car to exchange gifts. I got her a gray, fuzzy sweater that year. She made a "Lyndsay Kit," so she got me a tea steeper, and a couple of yoga shirts, and a gluten-free cookbook.

Going around the market we were talking, and everyone stopped us wherever we went; they wanted to see Tobi because she looked like a mini wolf. She was real tiny. We talked about how Car was feeling, and we were just trying on clothes, and being girls, and friends, and laughing. Carley said she was feeling pretty good then. She had just come back from Florida from Hippocrates. She was doing a new vegan diet, and she was really hoping that that would help, and she was saying, "My white blood cell count is back up, and I have a bit more energy and am feeling better," and she was really excited about having Tobi. She had always wanted a husky puppy, so she was really happy. She just always loved animals.

That was the last time I remember seeing Carley acting like herself, and then I think the cancer started spreading a lot more rapidly, and things started to change.

lotta love for this girl and my baby Tobi Bella
#lovemybaby #babytobi #lovemytobi ☺ ♥

CARLEY'S BLOG

Tobi-Bella
Posted on December 22, 2014

Hey Everyone!

I know it's been a really long time since I've blogged but I have an explanation! Things have gotten very busy in the Allison household! For starters ... I GOT A PUPPY! I've wanted a Pomsky for a very long time! Last Sunday I picked my little girl up from Air Canada Cargo and we've been having a great time ever since! She is twelve weeks old and only four pounds. I think getting Tobi is going to be the best thing for me. She's teaching me how to care for someone, while in turn helping me take the focus off my nausea and pain. She forces me to get fresh air and be more active. I honestly believe she is going to play a huge role in getting me better!

On another note! I am going to the studio on the 30th to record a cover song! I'm extremely excited but I have a lot of work to do in the next week! I will definitely be posting the song when it is all done! I'll be posting an update on how I've been feeling very soon!

I hope everyone is having a wonderful holiday season!

♥

Updates
Posted on December 29, 2014

Hey everyone!

So, I promised everyone an update on my health, and here it is! I have been feeling much better these days compared to the last couple months. I have lost a TON of weight so my chemotherapy pills have been adjusted, which has helped a lot! It really helped me understand why I was so sick on the chemo before. It was the standard adult dosage (since I am 19) but it was just too much for my body to handle. Now I am able to get up and out of the house so much more often than before. I am having a CT scan on January 5th and we are meeting with my oncologist on the 6th to get the results. I am very excited because I know we're going to get some good results! I can't feel the pain in my ribs before like I used to, and I truly think that means it's gone or almost gone.

I am SOOOO excited to record some music on Tuesday! I have decided to perform "Human" by Christina Perri, and I couldn't be more pumped. It's such a powerful song. I'm very excited to perform it.

Once it is all done I will be posting the final product! Can't wait!

JEFF ALLISON, Carley's cousin

She was very strong. I was very impressed with how strong she was. She was strong in a way that she could tackle having cancer and fight it. It didn't stop her. It didn't stop her, and she was amazing. The whole way through.

Every December, Carley's family and my family go up to Horton Tree Farm, just north of the city, for Christmas trees. We all share a lot of memories there. A lot of snowball fights and a lot of fun running around. In December 2014 she was very skinny; she had lost a lot of weight. She was all bundled up. There was no snow, but of course it was cold.

At the farm there is a rope swing with a big tire on it — it's old, very old — it's been there for years. And right away, Carley wanted to swing. Afterward both of us chose a tree; then, after having fun, we went by the fire. We had a hot chocolate and just chatted. She talked about how, if she couldn't go to university, she would like to take automotive courses so she could work with her mom. We just looked to the future.

Carley always had such an adventurous attitude, a daredevil attitude — whatever I was going to do, she wanted to do.

I don't go to the cliffs where we used to jump together anymore.

CARLEY'S BLOG

Happy New Year!
Posted on January 2, 2015

Happy New Year everyone!! Can't believe 2014 is over already, but I am ready for the new year, and ready to say goodbye to cancer once and for all! 2013 was the year every-thing changed. I fought tracheal clear cell sarcoma from February 4th 2013 - October 23rd 2013. 2014 was the year for recovery, and also the year my cancer came back. 2015 is going to be the year we say our final goodbyes to cancer.

I woke up this morning feeling pretty crappy. My mom came into my room to give me medications and I expressed to her that I was upset I was spending the first day of the new year in bed. So she told me the story of the year she spent New Year's Day in bed. It was the year I was born. January 1, 1996, my mom woke up with an awful cold; she couldn't get out of bed. She had previously decided that this would be the year she would try to qualify for the Olympics. She told herself she would start her training on January 1st. So when she woke up feeling awful she tried everything she could to get herself out of bed and running. But in the end she couldn't start her training that day and she had to let her body rest. And guess who made the Olympic team that Spring?! My momma! It goes to show that January 1st is just one day out of the entire year. It's about the decisions you make every single day.

I am confident that when 2016 rolls around, the cancer part of my life will be in the past. I know I have a lot of hard work ahead of me, but I'm excited to tackle it. I have been trying to do a little bit of physical activity a day to try and put on some muscle. Yesterday my mom bought a punching bag and boxing gloves! I can't wait to start using them! It's going to be the perfect way to get some exercise while getting all my anger out! Generally people with cancer have a build-up of anger, whether they know it or not. I've noticed in the last little while that deep down, I am angry about what's happened to me, and I think this will be the perfect way to deal with my anger.

♥

Boxing!
Posted on January 3, 2015

Finally had the energy to try out my boxing gloves and give the bag a few hits!

♥

Hey, Cancer, it's ass-kicking time

CT Scan Results

Posted on January 11, 2015

I hate making posts about bad news but it's bound to happen sometimes.

We got a call from my doctor the other day to inform us that the CT scan showed a spot in my left arm. Meaning my Cancer has spread to my left arm.

It's been extremely painful to move my arm and I need pain medication 24/7 to stay comfortable. I will be starting radiation on Tuesday to blast the Cancer in my arm. The protocol is the same as my lungs: five days of intensive radiation and then lots of recovery time. They say I shouldn't have many side effects other than some pain in my arm. Which is great, because I won't have to deal with nausea like last time.

I know this is a bit of a setback but we have a plan and we're gonna get through it just like every other bump in the road.

The CT Scan also showed much regression in the large tumor we were concerned about which is great!

But for now it's time to focus on blasting the Cancer in my arm and continue working on my lungs! Thank you everyone for always being there for me through everything! This has been a crazy journey and I'm looking forward to positive scans ahead!

MICHAEL NADEL, family friend

After her two performances at the Air Canada Centre, Carley Allison was approached by music producer Jon Levine, who produced songs for Rachel Platten, Bono and Selena Gomez. Carley performed Christina Perri's "Human" and the in-studio video was posted on YouTube. Levine's prologue to the video reads:

The voice you are about to hear is a miracle.

19-year-old Carley Allison wasn't supposed to be able to sing again after she had 5cm of her throat removed along with a cancerous tumor in 2013.

Carley is now fighting an inoperable kind of Lung Cancer called Clear Cell Sarcoma.

CARLEY'S YOUTUBE CHANNEL

Human by Christina Perri (cover by Carley Elle Allison)
www.youtube.com/watch?v=8rOwMjt_p70
372,105 views

Carley Allison
Published on 14 Jan 2015

I was given the wonderful opportunity to record with Jon Levine! Here is the progress of my voice! It's coming along! Hopefully getting back to where I was before surgery! Love you all.

CARLEY'S BLOG

Done Radiation 3.0
Posted on January 21, 2015

Finally done radiation for the third time!! My arm has increasingly developed more pain over the time period of radiation but we've been told that's a good sign! And it will start to feel better soon! I am SOOO excited to be leaving this deep freeze tomorrow morning and to arrive in sunny Sarasota FLORIDA!

I'm so lucky to be leaving this awful winter for a week and escaping to the warm with my dad and puppy Tobi! It's gonna be an amazing time to just relax and let myself heal. The salt water makes me feel 200 times better, and breathing in the moist air will hopefully help the congestion in my chest.

On another note I wanted to say a big thank you to everyone for the amount of support and kind words I got from all of you regarding my "Human" video!! It was such an amazing experience and I cannot thank all of you enough for the support. More music to come soon!!!!

Love you all xo

♥

Florida!

Posted on January 23, 2015

My dad, Tobi and I arrived in Florida and it's been nothing but sunshine since!! The weather has been incredible and we have been on the beach since the moment we got off the plane! The moist salty air here has been amazing for me and my cough is getting much better! I still have a lack of appetite, and lots of pain in my arm but I know by the end of the weekend I will really start feeling good!

I am so happy to be done with radiation in my arm and start treating my lungs again! We are busy trying to figure out what the next steps will be. We know the next decision we make will be an important one, so we have to make sure we've done all the research. My parents have been actively looking into treatments all over the world and I know they are going to find that one thing that will save me.

I'm excited to be spending the next week here but also excited to start working on some new music when I'm home!!

MARK ALLISON, Carley's dad

We decided to go to Florida, just Carley and me. And Tobi. And it was a fabulous trip. My brother's house that he let us use down there is beautiful. It's on the waterway. They had a boat, paddleboards, kayaks.

But Carley didn't do any of that. She just wasn't ... she was well enough to go out every day. We would get up in the morning ... she wanted to go to the beach. So, we took Tobi to the beach every morning, and we'd stay and get a cream cheese bagel, and she'd eat half of it. She wanted a new bathing suit. I told her whatever she wanted I would get her, so we just went into some bathing suit store in Sarasota and she saw one she liked, and I said, "Sure, get it," and she wore it while we were on the beach.

The weather was beautiful — warm blue skies. They say there are some of the nicest beaches in the world there. Pure white sand, and we were walking on the beach with a dog, and these people came by on these four-wheelers, and they said, "You're not allowed to have dogs on the beach — they'll fine you two hundred dollars."

Tobi was four months old; when we sat with her on the beach, she blended with the beach. So, we would sit far back in the sand and keep Tobi quiet.

I'm one to always grab the local paper whenever I go on vacation somewhere. I like to read what's happening locally. One day, I grabbed the paper — I think it was dropped at the front door — and I read that there was Daddy-Daughter night at a dinner theater — there was a dinner and a play, and I said,

#purebliss #nevercominghome

"Well, let's go." So, on Friday night, we got dressed up — she loved to get dressed up.

She put on one of these stick-on tattoos. It read FAITH.

There were twenty fathers and daughters there, and we bought a bunch of raffle tickets, and Carley won one of the prizes — puzzles and toys, which we ended up bringing home, and she gave them to John's nieces. She was so excited to bring this stuff home and give them to him.

The play was a musical, and it was just a really unique, fun thing, and the fact that it happened on the weekend that we were there was special.

Carley and I were in Florida for a week. Carley's cousin Jeffrey, my nephew, was there with us on Sunday, Monday, Tuesday, and we all came back on Wednesday. Once Jeffrey arrived, we used the boat. He took us to a little island. Carley and Jeffrey were having a great time on the beach there, and she was happy.

She loved that trip.

#cousins #funinthesun

JEFF ALLISON, Carley's cousin

I joined Mark, Carley and Tobi halfway through their week in Florida. In the mornings, she'd sleep until ten or eleven — we gave her the front room, overlooking the ocean. We'd spend some time at the house, just hanging out. We'd sit on the front balcony — there were a couple of chairs. We'd spend some time talking about what we were doing for the day and what the plans were, and Carley would explain to us what she wanted to do. She didn't always feel good — she was taking eighteen pills a day.

Once she felt good, we'd go out to the beach and spend some time on the beach. The sea air made her feel better, so we spent a lot of time there. And we took the boat out — just to experience the water. It was our last trip together.

MARK ALLISON, Carley's dad

Her doctor told Carley, against our wishes, that Carley was going to die. I left the doctor's office for a minute, and when I came back, Carley was crying.

CARLEY

I won't go there, not back to that room, not to the words the doctor told me. I'm going to show them. I am going to fight this. I am not going to let the doubts into my mind. I sit down to update my blog. This is where I can show my best self — the one that is not scared, the one that can inspire others to live their best lives. I put a smile on my face, and I begin to type.

CARLEY'S BLOG

Home!
Posted on January 29, 2015

I am officially home from Florida ... unfortunately. In ways I am happy to be home — I missed my family and home but I did not miss the cold Canadian Winter hahaha. The weather down there was incredible! Sunny and low of 75°F most days so it's safe to say we spent most of the time at the beach!

It was such a nice relaxing vacation and got to spend some much needed time in the sun!

We are home now and focusing on finding a new treatment. Finding treatments has been a very frustrating experience for my parents, and we are hoping the next treatment we choose will be a winner! Every time we start a treatment we are losing time, the next one has to work. My last scan showed some progression so we know we have to get this taken care of sooner than later.

It's hard sometimes to understand why we haven't found a cure, but I know we will find it soon!

We have to find it soon.

♥

Day 3
Posted on February 4, 2015

Hey everyone sorry I haven't been blogging much. Late Sunday night my arm really started hurting me, until it got so out of control that my parents called an ambulance. Once the paramedics got to my house, they came into the family room where I was lying down. Just my luck ... another student in training giving it a shot. I was so desperate for some medication that I just wanted them to get the IV in. The student was having so much trouble preparing the medication, we were halfway downtown before the IV was in. I know he was trying his best and just trying to do his job but at that point I was in so much pain I couldn't take it anymore.

After a long ambulance ride to the hospital, we get inside and would you look at that ... no rooms or beds available. So the paramedics for some reason left me in the stretcher right in front of the automatic sliding doors. So it's safe to say I was freezing after a couple minutes. After about an hour we were finally put in the room and I got to ask for pain medication, and do you know what they brought me? Advil. For someone who regularly has to take narcotics, Advil is just a joke.

The next day, I was transferred onto an in-patient ward. For some reason we couldn't get my pain under control. I was up every hour asking for more pain medication. I couldn't understand why they couldn't give me any more medication so I just had to toughen up and start dealing with the pain. The doctor came by to see me and saw how much pain I was in so he started to organize a team to get my surgery done soon. After A LOT of back and forth and A LOT of confusion, my surgery has been booked for tomorrow morning. I am so happy that something is finally being done about my arm. It has been such a frustrating week with a million different doctors, nurses, and pain medication protocols. But it's FINALLY over, and everything is set up for tomorrow.

The surgeon we got for my surgery happens to be the same doctor that operated on my auntie Caroline! (Not blood related, but she's my mom's best friend.) She had a very large tumor in her leg and this surgeon did an amazing job in fixing her all up! I'm confident he will get my arm all fixed and I can hopefully get back to living my life as "normal" as possible.

That's all for now. I will post an update (or someone will) after my surgery tomorrow!
Xoxoxo

♥

New Treatment Update

Posted on February 21, 2015

As I promised, I'm giving the results of my surgery. I'm sorry this has taken me so long but the recovery from surgery really was a challenge this time! I thought it would be a simple surgery just scraping the cancer from my bone and repairing it. But little did I know 70 stitches later and a bionic arm, it wasn't that simple!

However, thanks to my awesome surgeon, I think the arm is finally starting to recover!

Being in the hospital this time was definitely no walk in the park! The biggest difference was I was in an adult hospital.

Once my surgery was booked we were moved to Toronto General to have it done (but previously at Mt. Sinai). So now I can officially say I have been a patient in every hospital on University Avenue. Not something every nineteen-year-old can check off on their bucket list! The hospital stay was long but we are happy to be home now and I am happy to have the comfort of my own bed.

More on the medical side: the day we left the hospital it showed no cancer in my bones! Thank goodness! Then I had a spinal MRI because I had pain in my spine and that also came back clear. The cancer in my lungs is still progressing, however. We will be starting a new treatment on Monday! Wish me luck on our new treatment plans! I promise promise promise I actually mean it this time: I will keep everyone updated!

♥

New Carley's Angels Member
Posted on February 22, 2015

My Uncle Bruce has decided to join us in the ride this June! Such a big commitment since he and his family all live in BC. So excited to welcome Uncle Bruce onto the team and to be well enough to ride with everyone! Congratulations to everyone who has made a dent in their Fundraising!

Xoox

♥

Done chemo day one!
Posted on February 24, 2015

It's crazy to think that every time we said we wouldn't do more chemo, we just end up doing more chemo. This is a different kind of chemotherapy and is administered through

Naturopaths. It is given with a drug to protect your organs and decreases the side effects. So far I feel great! Hoping it stays this way! I will be having one week on, one week off, so next week I'm free!

MARK ALLISON, Carley's dad

We wanted to try everything we could, anything to save her. But we knew we were running out of time.

HOLLY DE JONGE, family friend

It was awful to see this disease take over this beautiful girl. Carley was frustrated, even angry, with the whole situation. She would be in so much pain, and there was nothing else the doctors could really do. May was incredible; she stopped working and was with Carley. I would go over a couple times a week. I would try to get Carley up and moving. I wanted her to think she could still do these normal activities, until it got really bad. We hung out a lot. We tried to stay positive the whole time, always giving her hope.

One time Carley said to me, "Tobi is going to have her own room soon."

I was lost for words. It was heartbreaking.

CARLEY

I'm in the music room, working on a song for John:

> *"I look into your eyes. It's hard to think we weren't here*
> *   before.*
> *When I see that smile, the one that shows me just how in*
> *   love you are … don't worry, everything will be all right."*

I don't like the next line so I scribble it out. Then I try:

> *"You stood by me … I don't know … what are these words.*
> *I don't know what to say. I just can't imagine things not*
> *   being this way.*
> *I want you to know … that I'm sorry. I tell you all the time.*
> *   You are mine. Only mine …"*

As I try to sing, my voice cracks. I take a deep breath. I'm not going to cry. I put a smile on my face and move away from the piano.

JOHN SERVINIS, Carley's boyfriend

She said she could never stay angry at me because I would smile. She sang to me a couple times. But she hated it because she thought I would judge her. She was always embarrassed about that, and then she wrote the song for me, and it took me so many months for me even to read the lyrics.

Carley and I went skating. I hadn't been skating in seven years, and Carley was just waiting to find the perfect day to convince me to go so she could make fun of me. I still don't know how to stop, but holding her hand and skating with her was probably one of the happiest moments we had together and was our last date together.

CARLEY'S BLOG

Chemo Week 2!
Posted on March 9, 2015

Here we are! Week Two of the safe chemo! I'm feeling good and excited for this week to get going. We're doing everything we can right now to kick cancer's butt!

On the weekend my hemoglobin dropped almost below 70 so I had to have a transfusion! Sunday we spent eight hours in North York General getting two bags of blood. I'm glad we did the transfusion because my body really felt like it needed it. I have much more energy today than I've had in a long time.

That's all the updates I have for now! xoxo

LYNDSAY REDDICK, Carley's friend

After a couple of weeks of me trying to come over but her having appointments, I texted her and said:

> I miss you, you're my best friend, I need to see you, so I don't care if you're just sleeping and you want to lie in bed. I'm coming to see you.

And she sent me a text and said:

> Okay, you can come.

She was in their living room. When she was sick, she would always sit on one of the big couches, and she was in a lot of pain, and she was taking a lot of painkillers. So, that was really hard for her and her family, and I didn't stay very long. Probably half an hour, and after I left, her sister said, "Carley isn't seeing anyone anymore. You, John and Sarah are the only people she's allowing into the house," which for me was — I knew that was the last turning point.

Very soon after that she was admitted into Princess Margaret again, and they tried to drain her lungs because they thought they were full of fluid, and when they drained her lungs, they found out it wasn't fluid — it was actually a mass. So, she was sent to palliative care at Princess Margaret.

CHAPTER TWELVE

I choose to smile,
and that's my triumph.

— Carley

LYNDSAY REDDICK, Carley's friend

Carley was in palliative care for about a week. There were no rules as to how many visitors. You can have as many people as you want whenever you want. There was a big lounge. I would go every day after college from around three o'clock in the afternoon to ten o'clock at night and then during the weekend. I remember it was all the friends and the family. My sister and I were there every day. Carley's parents and her sisters and John were there every day. One of Riley's friends, Natalie, was there every day, and then other friends would come and go, because a lot of friends came over from university to see her, and then her aunts and uncles would come and go. So, we would all hang out in the lounge together, and take turns going into her room and seeing her and talking to her. On Sunday she had been very spotty. Like, she was on a lot of sedatives and painkillers, so she wasn't herself, and then on Sunday everyone left her room and let her and John just talk and be together.

My sister and I were trying to find a music room for her

because we wanted her sister Riley to play the guitar for her, and she called us in as we were walking past her room, and I remember she was coherent, and we had ten minutes where she was coherent, and it was just her, John and my sister and me, and we got ten minutes to talk, and we were talking about how she never stopped believing that she was going to be okay. We were talking about what we were going to do when she got out of the hospital, and all the things that she was excited for, and how she couldn't wait to not be sick anymore. That was who she was. She always believed that she was going to get better and she was going to get back to her old life. She just always had such a positive outlook, even when she was so sick. So, to me that was just a very significant moment in our friendship, and really solidified who she was.

She wanted to sing again, and we were going to ride horses, and she was going to go back to school. She was going to be able to play the guitar again. Just, like, all the things that she loved, and all the small things that she got to do every day that she couldn't anymore.

DAN ALLISON, Carley's cousin

Carley was always concerned about other people. In her hospital room, if you were upset, she asked you to leave. She didn't want that kind of energy in there; she was very specific about it. I'm not particularly overly emotional myself, but when I walked up to the room for the first time, I broke down and immediately just went down the hallway. I had my moment with Mark and May, and then I came back and was fine. She loved eating watermelon Popsicles. I think she pretty much ate watermelon Popsicles that entire week.

I got off all my exams because we heard that she was terminal at that point, and Carley said to me, "Dan, go back. Go back to school. Get out of here. Like, you don't need to be here." Right. 'Cause in her mind, she's so positive. She's thinking, Nope, I've got this. I can beat this. Like with everything else I'll just blow my way through it.

And it was incredible. She spent all her energy and remaining time making sure everybody else was okay. It was the most courageous show of strength that I've ever seen in any person.

SARAH FISHER, Carley's friend

The last time I saw Carley was in palliative care. She had the same Carley brightness she always had, and at that point she had so much medication that it was difficult for her to sit up and to do certain things, but with Carley being Carley, everyone who came to visit was telling funny stories, everyone was laughing. In her room, she had a big, beautiful window that looked out onto the street, and it was really nice outside. There was sun, and it felt like anywhere Carley was, was bright always.

One of the last things we did was put her computer on the table so we could put some singing show on. But I thought something was missing. I thought it was music, so we wanted to bring in some sort of music, and I remember Carley started to put her arm up to reach out. And everyone looked at Riley, who was Carley's second hands. Riley knew what Carley needed without Carley having to say anything.

Riley said to me, "Fish, I think she wants you."

And Carley had her hand out, so I held her hand, and we sort of held hands and just — again, the most unbelievable thing as we were holding hands: she moved her thumb back and forth, so she was almost comforting me. It didn't matter how she was feeling or what she was going through. She was thinking, How can I make you feel better? And that was a really wonderful moment for us. That I'll remember forever.

I'll remember her strength, too. Cancer never, ever took away her smile, her laughter, her brightness, her personality. It never took Carley away.

SAM SERVINIS, John's mom

John's dad, Gus, had been diagnosed with cancer, and he was at the same hospital Carley was at for her care. We weren't sure how critical the situation was for Carley because it was a sudden, real sudden downfall — like, really quickly. On Monday, she suddenly supposedly got this burst of energy and was, like, "I need to go now to see Gus." Carley and her family were waiting for us to say, "Okay, he's in the room, getting his chemo. Come down."

She was trying to get up by herself. Meanwhile, she had no strength in her, so they carried her into the wheelchair, and then she came downstairs. And she was awake and alert suddenly, and she wanted ... she wanted to see Gus, like suddenly she became so aware, and you wouldn't think two minutes ago she was so fragile, like beyond; and she still looked fragile — don't get me wrong — but she just wanted to be there for him. That day she had to see Gus she wanted her hair fully brushed and she wanted Athena, my daughter, to do her nails.

In those last days she wanted to eat stuff. I brought penne alla vodka; she wanted penne alla vodka. She loved my penne alla vodka.

I remember that night. Riley was playing the guitar, and we had gone in to visit Carley. It was the end of the song, and Carley was, like, basically half asleep, doped, right, from the medication, so we thought she wasn't listening. But still they were singing the song.

And at the end of it I said, "Oh, Carley probably doesn't know, but John played the electric guitar when he was a kid, and he took lessons."

And then suddenly Carley wakes up, and her eyes are open, and she smiles. And she says, "Stop, you're killing me." That's all she said, and then she closed her eyes again with a smirk. She thought that was so funny.

LYNDSAY REDDICK, Carley's friend

On her last night, someone had brought a guitar, so someone convinced Riley to play the guitar. Riley played a Taylor Swift song. "Sparks Fly." Riley sang and played, and she finished and Car said, "That was really good, Ri, good job."

And Ri said, "Thanks, Car. Why don't you sing for me."

And Car said, "I can't, Ri. I can't do it anymore. You have to sing alone."

JOHN SERVINIS, Carley's boyfriend

The last thing Carley ever said to me was "Oh, I'll see you tomorrow, love you." That's it.

CHAPTER THIRTEEN

Always smile.

— Carley

CARLEY'S BLOG

Posted on March 31, 2015

Hi Everyone,

It's guest bloggers Riley (Carley's Big Sister) and John (Carley's Boyfriend). This time the guest blog is not one that anyone is going to want to read.

After a hard week in the hospital, this morning Carley passed away.

She left memories and a legacy that will live on forever in our hearts and minds. She never quit fighting until her last breath; she showed more strength than anyone thought was possible. Unfortunately, this disease is not one to discriminate the evil from the good, the greedy from the giving, the cold-hearted from the kind-hearted. She was nothing less than an angel that spread her smile, joy, and charismatic nature to everyone around her. There was nothing she would have wanted more than for the people she loved to be happy. So reflect and reminisce on how she touched you and the inspiration, bravery and joy she brought into your life. Her life may have been short, but the number of lives she was able to touch and inspire is unparalleled to some people that have lived vast amounts of years.

On top of being an inspiring soul, Carley was a sister, daughter and girlfriend whose unconditional love will never be replaced. This situation is one that is hard to talk about for anyone that had been close to her, and any one of us could go on for hours, but the words would still never be enough to describe and honor this remarkable and inde-scribable person. This may be the last post on this blog, to leave her memories and words untouched. However, we are in the midst of creating a foundation to continue and honor her legacy, journey, and fight to inspire youth and people of all walks of life to keep fighting and find a cure to this disease that has taken another angel.

May she be blissful in your memories and always with you in your heart.

SAMANTHA ALLISON, Carley's sister

Carley never wanted people to think of her life as a tragedy. She wanted people to be happy that it happened, rather than sad that it ended.

From **NATALIE BEATON**'s funeral speech, **RILEY**'s best friend

"People are always amazed by the amount of strength that Carley showed in her journey, always working to beat what was put in front of her. Anyone who has ever been in a competition with Carley can understand exactly where this comes from. She was probably the most competitive kid there was, and wanted to beat everyone and everything that stood in her way from winning. Riley and I used to always joke about how we hated running with her because Carley always had to be one step ahead of you. For a couple of summers, we formed a running club beginning when Riley and I were fourteen, so Carley would have been around twelve. It was me, Riley, Carley, my older sister Samantha. Of course our club was led by the Olympian marathon runner May. May always pushed us to run as hard as we could, but you would always find Riley and I laughing about something in the back. But up in the front would always be Carley, battling tooth and nail with my sixteen-year-old sister Sam to be first place in a recreational summer run.

I remember in middle school we had a school-wide Terry Fox race that was five kilometers. I was in grade nine, and Carley was in grade seven. We ran together and crossed the finish line at the exact same time. The only reason she didn't beat me handily was because I was two years older than her, five inches taller than her and desperate to not lose to my best friend's little sister. But that race pretty much summed up Carley. There was no competition too stiff for her, and she always, always wanted to be just that little bit ahead.

But I have to say that some of my fondest memories with Carley have come from spending time at their cottage. This is the place where Carley really showcased how fearless she was.

I can't stand up here and say anything that will make sense of what has happened. But what I will say is in nineteen short years, Carley was lucky to have fallen in love with the most kind-hearted boy, John. She had the most dedicated father, most supportive mother, who were at every talent show, sporting event, birthday party. She had the most amazing older sister a girl can ask for, who she got to do everything with, look up to. And lastly, she got to be the big sister to the sweetest little sister in the world, who idolized her. She was unconditionally loved. She left her mark on this world.

Carley, you will always be my little sister. I love you, and I will miss you."

CHAPTER FOURTEEN

PAUL ALOFS, President and CEO, the Princess Margaret Cancer Foundation

At the 2015 Ride to Conquer Cancer, a tribute video of Carley singing the national anthem was played to open the Ride and to celebrate Carley's life. Carley was taken from us way too soon but left such a powerful and positive impression on everyone who had the good fortune to meet her. Mark Allison, Carley's dad, did a heroic job introducing the tribute video, and then he and his wife, May, and extended family of about thirty did the Ride. We all have a reason that we ride in this transformational event. But we also all have a "who" we ride for. My wife, Sheila, and I rode in memory of the wonderful Carley Allison, along with our own family members who we always ride for. Carley inspires all of us, and we are all so much better off having known her.

LYNDSAY REDDICK, Carley's friend

I so clearly remember the first day Carley and I met, and I think she just had a personality that people were drawn to. Like, you met Carley, and you knew she was in the room, and you could sense her energy, and she always had so much energy, and she was always up for anything, and she was really adventurous, and she was just sassy and fun, but she was no bullshit at the same time. She wasn't afraid to tell you how she really felt or what she really thought. So, she just had an energy that I think drew people to her, and I think that's why people are so drawn to her story. They can sense that energy, maybe.

I think people really connect with the struggle, and how she overcame it, and how open she was about it. Like, on her blog and on her Instagram she has posts saying it was shitty this happened, "but I'm smiling. It's going to be okay," so I think people connect to both her struggle and her positive outlook and resiliency.

MARK ALLISON, Carley's dad

I don't think we ever move on.

But we have found comfort. Riley was the first one to tell us about something called Dimes from Heaven. Riley brought it to us because one of her professors at university told her that she might start finding dimes. Somehow, Carley would leave them for us. Within two weeks, those dimes started coming along. We started finding them, although it just doesn't seem possible, but sometimes when you really need one, you find one. We have so many now.

MAY and MARK ALLISON, Carley's parents

MAY: I find our extended family is closer because of Carley's situation. I find our relationships are stronger in a lot of ways, and I think that was all happening as ... when Carley was getting sick. And I think it has to do with how she brought us all together.

MARK: We ended up spending a lot of time together, and now we do a lot of things. Like we have these events, you know — we have the Cycle for Carley and the Concert for Carley. We do the Ride to Conquer Cancer. Every year. We have raised a lot of money this way.

SAMANTHA ALLISON, Carley's sister

Carley really wanted to wear the first dress that she bought to her prom. It's a silver dress, with one shoulder, and it's tight, with a slit.

I remember Carley saying, "I'm so excited for prom. I'm so excited to wear my dress."

I thought she would've wanted someone to wear it to their prom.

I remember I got my makeup done, then I came home and put on Carley's prom dress. It zipped up the side. I don't have a mirror in my room, and I went to look in the mirror. I saw myself, and my hair is a little bit blonder in the summer. So, I looked in there, and I thought, I look like Carley. Then I walked downstairs, and Riley was standing in the kitchen. And my dad had a camera. And Riley hugged me and cried a little bit. I told them not to cry.

I wore Carley's dress to my prom that night. That was really special for me.

JOHN SERVINIS, Carley's boyfriend

Carley motivated me. She realigned me. Before, in high school, I didn't really care about school that much. Sure, I did well in school, but I just didn't care that much. When I was with her, I saw my future, and I knew I had to do this, because otherwise I couldn't get the life I wanted with her or be able to achieve my dreams. I wanted to travel with her and stuff.

When we talked about the future, we already dealt with her working at the dealerships, me doing dentistry, and then we were going to visit my family in Greece. She wanted to do that really badly, because most of my family is there. She wanted to actually learn a bit of Greek. She'd try and listen because she wanted to understand my grandparents more.

I have a book that she made that's *Things I Love About You.* I know from that that she loved that I made her smile.

I think she brought me a more realistic perspective. She was the one person who always was determined that I would get into dentistry and do this and do that. And she believed it, even when I had my doubts all the time because the chances are so slim.

The day of my interview I found two dimes as I was walking out of the hall from the interview. So that was huge. I didn't think I could love anyone as much as I loved Carley. It was the type of love that made me believe that two souls could be aligned. Our love story may seem like a tragedy, but these were the happiest moments in my life; she made me realize that.

RILEY ALLISON, Carley's sister

Due to the rareness of Carley's cancer, traditional medicine alone was not enough. Instead we searched for a combination of traditional and holistic treatments that would help Carley. The holistic treatments proved to be specifically helpful to Carley during her journey. However, these holistic treatments were not available in hospital and proved difficult to access. Because of this, we are working to unite holistic and traditional cancer care to make these holistic treatments accessible to cancer patients and their families, all while spreading Carley's message of Always Smile.

At Carley's Angels we do a variety of different things to raise money. The first thing we did was jewelry. My friend Natalie decided that she was going to get us matching necklaces with the words *Always Smile* because that was Carly's motto. We figured that we were going to help raise money for Carley's Angels by making this jewelry, and you get it in the shop in our backyard with, like, four or five of us stringing things together and stamping each letter individually on these pieces of sterling silver and stainless steel. At our first event we sold out in thirty minutes — all two hundred pieces or something crazy. Now we make jewelry and sell it online to raise money for the foundation, but we also do a multitude of events.

The necklaces remind me of a day when Carley and I were sitting on the couch. It was where we hung out when she wasn't feeling good, and I have a necklace from my grandpa that he got for my grandma, and it had *I love you* stamped on it, and we always said it was such a cool necklace. We always said we'd really love to remake the necklace, and so that day I ordered the stamps, and we tried to make Tobi a collar, and we could barely fit Tobi's name on it. It was terrible. The name has four letters. It took twelve tries.

Carley had so many passions that she was involved with on a daily basis. Singing and skating were her first loves — and when we had to watch those being taken away from her, we learned that we can't take anything for granted. Yet for some reason, even with her voice and her ability to skate being taken away from her, she was still telling us to always smile.

ALICE KUIPERS, author

It has been an honor to witness Carley's story and to turn it into this book — hopefully, Carley continues to inspire many more people to live the way she lived.

Cancer did not beat Carley. It never won. It only made her stronger. It made her light shine more brightly.

CARLEY

It's not about how long you live,
but how you spend the time while you are alive.

Always be the best you can be.

Enjoy those you love.

Happiness is found in the day-to-day.
It is found in the smile of someone who loves you.

It's life, and we have to enjoy it as it is.

Keep trying, because next time you might succeed.

Scars are reminders of the life you have lived.

It's about the decisions you make every single day.

Even in the darkest days, it is a beautiful life.

Live each day to the most, because life is not very long.

I've never been stronger than I am right now.

I choose to smile, and that's my triumph.

Always smile.

ALICE KUIPERS is an award-winning, bestselling author of five YA novels, two picture books and a chapter book series. Her work has been published in 32 countries. She lives in Saskatoon, Saskatchewan, with the writer Yann Martel and their four children. Find out more about her and join her free online writing course here: **alicekuipers.com**